LIFE and HEALTH
Insurance License Exam Prep

The Straight-to-the-Point Training Book, with 10 Complete and Up-to-Date Practice Tests, to Help You Easily Pass the Exam on Your First Try

Adam James Scott

TABLE OF CONTENTS

INTRODUCTION

Welcome to your comprehensive resource for navigating the intricate path toward earning your Life and Health Insurance License. This guide has been meticulously crafted to give you the essential knowledge, strategies, and confidence to excel in the challenging journey of preparing for and conquering the licensing exam.

Life and health insurance are vital pillars of financial security and well-being in today's ever-changing landscape. Becoming a licensed insurance professional opens the door to a fulfilling career where you can profoundly affect individuals' lives by guiding them toward making informed decisions to protect their futures.

This guide is designed to be your unwavering companion as you prepare for the exam, offering a clear roadmap through the diverse subjects and concepts that form the foundation of the insurance industry. From the fundamentals to the intricacies, from ethical considerations to regulatory frameworks, we have curated the content to ensure you are well-equipped for success.

"Life and Health Insurance License Exam Guide" covers a spectrum of topics crucial to understanding the insurance landscape, ensuring you have a holistic grasp of the field.

Complex ideas are demystified through concise explanations, real-life examples, and relatable scenarios, helping you bridge the gap between theory and application.

Our content is aligned with the specific requirements of the Life and Health Insurance License Exam, presenting essential concepts, terminology, and strategies tailored to maximize your exam performance.

Reinforce your learning with practice questions that mirror the exam's format and difficulty level, allowing you to fine-tune your skills and gauge your progress.

Gain insights into effective test-taking strategies, time management, and approaches to different question types, empowering you to navigate the exam confidently.

Upholding ethical standards is paramount in the insurance industry. We explore ethical principles and considerations, ensuring you are prepared to uphold professionalism and integrity.

As you embark on this transformative journey with the "Life and Health Insurance License Exam Guide," you are preparing for an exam and laying the foundation for a rewarding career. This guide is your compass, providing you with the tools and knowledge needed to succeed on the exam and make a lasting impact in the world of life and health insurance. Let us embark on this voyage, unlocking your potential and paving the way for a prosperous future as a licensed insurance professional.

CHAPTER 1:
The Life and Health Examination in the USA

The life and health insurance exam is a significant milestone for individuals aspiring to become licensed insurance professionals in the United States. This chapter delves into key aspects of the exam, including eligibility criteria, the number of questions, and the diverse requirements set by different states for the life and health insurance examination.

1.1 Who Is Eligible to Take the Exam?

Eligibility to sit for the life and health insurance exam is determined by specific criteria established by state insurance departments. While these criteria may vary slightly from state to state, there are common prerequisites that candidates need to meet:

- **Minimum Age:** Typically, candidates must be at least 18 to be eligible for the Examination.

- **Pre-Licensing Education:** Many states require candidates to complete a pre-licensing education course covering fundamental life and health insurance concepts.

- **Background Check:** Candidates may be subject to a background check as part of the licensing process to ensure their suitability for the insurance profession.

- **Application and Fees:** Aspiring insurance professionals are usually required to submit an application and pay an examination fee to the relevant state insurance department.

- **Residency Requirements:** Some states may have residency requirements or mandate that candidates be U.S. citizens or legal residents.

It is important to note that state insurance departments have the authority to regulate licensing requirements, resulting in variations in eligibility criteria. As such, prospective candidates should thoroughly review and understand the specific requirements outlined by their state's insurance department.

1.2 Number of Questions

The number of life and health insurance exam questions can vary based on the state and the exam provider. Generally, the exam consists of multiple-choice questions designed to assess the candidate's understanding of insurance principles, policies, regulations, and ethical considerations. While the exact count of questions may differ, a typical life and health insurance exam may include approximately 150 to 200 questions.

Candidates should be well prepared to address questions across various topics, including insurance fundamentals, different policy types, underwriting procedures, policy provisions, ethical considerations, and more. The questions evaluate the candidate's knowledge and ability to apply insurance concepts in real-world scenarios.

1.3 State Requirements for Life and Health Exams

Each state within the United States has specific life and health insurance exam requirements. These requirements may include:

- **Pre-Licensing Education:** Many states mandate certain pre-licensing education hours that candidates must complete before being eligible to take the exam. This education provides essential knowledge required for proficiency in the insurance field.

- **Licensing Fees:** Candidates must pay an examination fee during the application process. This fee covers administrative expenses associated with conducting the Examination.

- **Passing Score:** Candidates must achieve a designated passing score on the exam to obtain their insurance license. The state insurance department determines the passing score.

- **Background Check and Fingerprints:** Certain states require candidates to undergo a background check and provide fingerprints as part of the licensing process, ensuring the fitness of candidates for the insurance profession.

- **Residency or Citizenship Requirements:** Some states may impose residency or citizenship prerequisites that candidates must fulfill to qualify for licensure.

For a comprehensive understanding of the specific life and health insurance exam requirements in a particular state, candidates should refer to the official website of their state's insurance department. This valuable resource will provide detailed guidance on prerequisites, application procedures, exam content, and other pertinent information.

In summary, the life and health insurance exam constitutes a crucial step toward obtaining licensure as an insurance professional in the United States. Eligibility criteria, the number of questions, and state-specific conditions collectively shape a candidate's journey to take and successfully pass the Examination. Prospective insurance professionals should diligently research and comprehend the requirements stipulated by their state's insurance department to ensure a seamless and triumphant examination process.

CHAPTER 2:
Forms of Life Policies

Life insurance is a fundamental tool in personal finance, providing individuals with a means to protect their loved ones and secure their financial future. This chapter delves into the intricate world of life insurance, exploring the basics, various types of policies, and innovative combinations that cater to diverse needs. By comprehensively understanding life insurance basics, whole life insurance, term life insurance, types of annuities, and combination plans, individuals can make informed decisions that align with their unique circumstances.

2.1 Life Insurance Fundamentals

Life insurance is based on the principle of risk management. It is a contract between a policyholder and an insurance company where the policyholder agrees to pay regular premiums for a lump-sum payment, referred to as the mortality benefit, this payment is made to beneficiaries after the insured's passing. The chapter begins by laying the groundwork for life insurance, defining key concepts such as policyholder, insured, beneficiaries, and premiums. It highlights the significance of life insurance as a safety net that protects families from financial hardship in the event of the insured's untimely death. By internalizing these fundamental ideas, readers can comprehend the significance of life insurance in providing financial security and peace of mind.

2.2 Whole Life Insurance

Whole life insurance, or permanent life insurance, is all-inclusive coverage that lasts the insured's entire lifespan. This part explores the characteristics and advantages of whole life insurance policies. The cash value component, which develops over time as policyholders pay premiums, is one of its defining characteristics. This cash value can be withdrawn or used as collateral, providing liquidity and financial flexibility. The paragraph also emphasizes permanent life insurance's predictability and long-term security, with its fixed premiums and guaranteed mortality benefit. In addition, the potential for dividends increases the policy's value and provides policy growth opportunities.

2.3 Term Life Insurance

Unlike permanent life insurance, term life insurance covers a specified period. This part examines the features of term life insurance, focusing on its affordability and suitability for temporary requirements. Term policies are frequently used to protect against specific financial obligations, such as mortgage payments or income replacement during financially vulnerable years for dependents. The section also emphasizes term insurance's renewable and convertible characteristics, which allow policyholders to extend coverage or convert to a permanent policy as their circumstances change. Although term insurance lacks the financial value component of permanent insurance, its simplicity and affordability make it an attractive option for many people.

2.4 Types of Annuities

Another crucial aspect of financial planning, annuities provide a steady income source during retirement. This segment examines annuities and contractual agreements between individuals and insurance companies. Annuities can be classified as either immediate, in which payments commence shortly after the contract is established, or deferred, in which payments are scheduled for a later date.

There are various forms of annuities, such as:

- Fixed annuities, that provide a stable, predetermined income.
- Variable annuities tied to investment performance.
- Indexed annuities that offer growth potential based on market indexes.

Annuities provide individuals with a valuable instrument for securing a steady income stream and ensuring retirement financial security.

2.5 Combination Plans

The final part explores innovative solutions combining life insurance and annuities elements. These combination plans are designed for individuals who desire comprehensive financial strategies. This portion features hybrid products that combine life insurance and annuities to address specific requirements, such as survivorship policies that cover two lives and payout upon the second death. Joint-life insurance may appeal to couples seeking shared protection. In addition, variations such as modified endowment contracts (MECs) offer policyholders flexible options to fulfill their specific financial objectives. This paragraph emphasizes the adaptability and customization inherent in contemporary insurance products, which enable individuals to tailor coverage to their particular circumstances.

CHAPTER 3:

Provisions, Options, Riders, and Exclusions in Life Policy

3.1 Policy Riders

Policy riders can be added to a life insurance policy to customize it and enhance its coverage according to the policyholder's specific needs. These riders offer flexibility and allow individuals to tailor their policies to better suit their circumstances.

Various types of policy riders are available, each serving a unique purpose. Some common types include:

1. **Accelerated Death Benefit Rider:** This rider allows policyholders to access a portion of the death benefit if diagnosed with a terminal illness. It provides financial support during a challenging time.

2. **Waiver of Premium Rider:** In case of disability, this rider waives premium payments, ensuring that the policy remains in force while the insured cannot work.

3. **Long-Term Care Rider:** This rider provides coverage for long-term care expenses, such as nursing home care, using a portion of the death benefit.

4. **Critical Illness Rider:** If the insured is diagnosed with a critical illness like cancer or heart disease, this rider offers a lump-sum payout to cover medical expenses.

5. **Accidental Death Benefit Rider:** This clause provides an additional benefit in the event of the insured's death due to an accident., providing extra financial protection for beneficiaries.

Policy riders offer several advantages, including:

1. **Customization:** Riders allow policyholders to tailor their coverage to their needs and life circumstances.

2. **Flexibility:** As life situations change, riders provide the flexibility to adjust coverage without needing a new policy.

3. **Comprehensive Coverage:** Riders can extend coverage to scenarios not covered by the base policy, like critical illnesses or long-term care needs.

4. **Cost-Effectiveness:** Adding riders to an existing policy is often more cost-effective than purchasing separate coverage for specific needs.

When considering policy riders, evaluating individual needs and potential risks is important. Working with a licensed insurance professional can help individuals decide which rider best aligns with their goals and circumstances. Overall, policy riders enhance the value and versatility of life insurance policies, offering tailored benefits and additional layers of protection for policyholders and their beneficiaries.

3.2 Policy Provisions

Policy provisions are the essential terms and conditions outlined in a life insurance contract that establish the rights, responsibilities, and obligations of the insurance company and the policyholder. These provisions ensure that the policy operates as intended and clarify how it functions over its duration.

Some important policy provisions include:

1. **Insuring Clause:** This provision states the insurer's promise to pay a death benefit to the beneficiary upon the insured's death. It outlines the basic purpose of the policy.

2. **Grace Period:** The grace period is a period following the insurance premium due date during which the policy remains active, even if the premium has not yet been paid. The unpaid premium will be deducted from the benefit in the event of the insured's death during this period.

3. **Incontestability Clause:** After a certain period (typically two years) from the policy issue date, the insurer cannot contest the policy's validity or deny a claim based on misstatements in the application.

4. **Suicide Clause:** This provision typically states that if the insured dies by suicide within a certain period after the policy is issued (often two years), the death benefit will not be paid, and the premiums paid will be refunded.

5. **Policy Loans:** Many whole life insurance policies allow policyholders to take out loans against the policy's cash value. The policy provisions specify the terms and conditions for these loans, including interest rates and repayment terms.

6. **Dividend Options:** The provision outlines how policyholders can receive dividends for participating policies. Common options include using dividends to purchase additional coverage, receive cash, accumulate interest, or repay policy loans.

7. **Change of Beneficiary:** This provision outlines the process for changing the policy's designated beneficiary and may require written consent from the current beneficiary.

8. **Assignment:** The policyholder may assign ownership or rights of the policy to another party. This provision details the process and requirements for such assignments.

9. **Nonforfeiture Options:** If the policyholder discontinues premium payments, nonforfeiture options allow the policy to retain some value. Common options include cash surrender value, reduced paid-up, and extended-term insurance.

10. **Settlement Options:** This provision outlines how the death benefit can be paid to the beneficiary, such as lump-sum payment, installments, or an annuity.

3.3 Life Policy Options

Life insurance policy options allow policyholders to customize their coverage to better suit their circumstances and financial goals. These options allow policyholders to enhance their coverage, adjust premium payments, and utilize the policy's benefits to align with their needs. Here are some common life policy options:

1. **Waiver of Premium Rider:** If the insured person becomes disabled & unable to work, this option will not require premium payments. It ensures that the policy remains in force during times of financial hardship.

2. **Accidental Death Benefit Rider:** If the insured dies due to an accident, this rider provides an additional death benefit on top of the base policy's benefit. It can help provide extra financial protection for the insured's beneficiaries.

3. **Guaranteed Insurability Rider:** The policyholder can purchase additional coverage at specified intervals without undergoing a medical exam. It is valuable for individuals who anticipate needing more coverage in the future.

4. **Term Conversion Rider:** For term life insurance policies, this option allows the policyholder to convert the policy into a permanent life insurance policy without undergoing a medical exam. It provides flexibility as life circumstances change.

5. **Accelerated Death Benefit Rider:** In certain situations, if the insured has been diagnosed as having a terminal disease, this rider enables them to obtain a part of the death reward while still alive. It may improve life quality or assist in paying for medical costs.

6. **Child Term Rider:** This option provides a small amount of life insurance coverage for the policyholder's children, typically cheaply. It helps alleviate funeral expenses if the unthinkable happens.

7. **Flexible Premium Payment Options:** Some policies offer flexibility in premium payments, allowing the policyholder to adjust the premium amount and payment frequency to accommodate changing financial situations.

8. **Return of Premium Rider:** With this rider, if the insured outlives the policy term, a portion or all of the premiums paid are returned to the policyholder. It provides savings if the insured does not pass away during coverage.

Life policy options enable policyholders to tailor their insurance coverage to their unique needs, ensuring they receive the maximum benefits from their policies. Before choosing any options, it is essential for policyholders to thoroughly understand the terms, costs, and potential benefits associated with each option. Consulting with an insurance professional can help policyholders make well-informed decisions about which options best align with their financial goals and circumstances.

3.4 Policy Exclusions

Policy exclusions are specific situations or circumstances outlined in a life insurance policy where the insurer may deny or limit coverage. While life insurance is designed to provide financial protection to beneficiaries, certain risks and scenarios may be excluded to manage the insurer's risk and maintain the policy's affordability. Here are some common policy exclusions:

1. **Suicide Clause:** Many life insurance policies include a suicide clause that limits coverage if the insured dies by suicide within a specified period after the policy's issuance. Typically, if the insured dies by suicide within the first one to two years of the policy, the death benefit may be limited to a return of premiums paid.

2. **Misrepresentation or Fraud:** The insurer may deny a claim if the insured provides false information or withholds important details during the application process. Providing accurate and honest information is crucial to ensure the policy remains valid.

3. **Dangerous Activities:** High-risk activities such as extreme sports, skydiving, or racing may limit coverage or exclusions. Suppose the insured participates in such activities and passes away. As a result, the insurer might deny the claim.

4. **War and Acts of Terrorism:** Some policies may not cover death resulting from war, terrorism, or other conflicts. These exclusions help insurers manage the increased risks associated with these events.

5. **Criminal Activities:** The policy may not provide coverage if the insured dies while participating in criminal activities or if the death results from illegal actions.

6. **Aviation Exclusion:** Sometimes, life insurance won't pay out if you die while flying in a private plane.

Policy exclusions are explicitly stated in the insurance contract to ensure clarity and transparency for the policyholder and the insurer. It is essential for policyholders to thoroughly review and understand the exclusions outlined in their policies. While exclusions may limit coverage in certain situations, they help maintain the integrity of the insurance pool and keep premiums affordable for all policyholders. Policyholders should work closely with their insurance agents or advisors to fully comprehend policy exclusions and make informed decisions about their coverage.

CHAPTER 4:
Other Life Insurance Definitions

Life insurance is a multifaceted financial tool that extends beyond providing a safety net for beneficiaries. In this chapter, we delve into essential concepts related to retirement planning, taxes, beneficiaries, life settlements, and group life insurance. Understanding these concepts is crucial for making informed decisions about life insurance and its role in comprehensive financial planning.

4.1 Life Insurance Contract Elements

The life insurance contract is an agreement between the insurance company and the policyholder and is legally binding. It sets out the terms and conditions of the cover, the rights of the insured, and the responsibilities of both parties. The key elements of life insurance contracts include:

1. **Offer and Acceptance:** The insurance company offers coverage based on the information provided by the applicant, and the applicant accepts the terms by paying the first premium.

2. **Consideration:** The premium payments made by the policyholder constitute the consideration for the insurance company's promise to provide coverage.

3. **Legal Purpose:** The contract must have a lawful purpose, and both parties must enter into it with the intent to create a legal obligation.

4. **Competent Parties:** Both the policyholder and the insurance company must have the legal capacity to enter into a contract.

5. **Mutual Agreement:** Both parties must agree on the terms and conditions of the policy, including coverage amount, premium payments, and beneficiaries.

6. **Conditional Contract:** The insurance company's obligation to pay the death benefit is contingent upon the occurrence of the insured's death within the policy's terms.

7. **Representations and Warranties:** The policyholder's application is considered a representation of the information provided and must be accurate and truthful.

8. **Insurable Interest:** The policyholder must have a valid interest in the insured's life, typically required to prevent speculative insurance purchases.

9. **Entire Contract Clause:** The policy, application, and any attached riders constitute the contract between the parties.

Understanding these elements ensures policyholders are well-informed about their contractual rights and responsibilities.

4.2 Retirement Plans

Retirement planning is a critical component of financial preparedness. Life insurance can play a significant role in retirement strategies, complementing other retirement savings vehicles. Here are ways life insurance can be integrated into retirement planning:

- **Annuities:** Annuities are insurance products that offer a guaranteed income stream in retirement. They can provide a stable source of funds to cover living expenses, especially for those concerned about outliving their savings.

- **Cash Value Policies:** Permanent life insurance policies, including whole life and universal life, build cash value over time. During retirement, policyholders can utilize this cash value to supplement additional sources of income.

- **Tax Benefits:** Certain life insurance policies offer tax advantages, such as tax-deferred growth and tax-free withdrawals, which can be advantageous in retirement planning.

- **Estate Planning:** Life insurance can play a role in estate planning, ensuring that beneficiaries receive a tax-efficient inheritance and that estate taxes are covered.

Individuals can create a more comprehensive and diversified retirement strategy by incorporating life insurance into retirement planning.

4.3 Life Settlement

A life settlement is a financial transaction in which a policyholder sells his or her life insurance policy to a third party in exchange for a payment made in a lump sum. Individuals who no longer need or can afford their life insurance coverage typically consider this option. The third party becomes the new owner of the policy and assumes responsibility for premium payments. Upon the insured's passing, the new owner receives the death benefit.

Key points about life settlements include:

- **Vertical Settlements:** Vertical settlements are a specific type of life settlement in which the policyholder has a terminal or chronic illness. Vertical settlements provide financial assistance to individuals facing significant medical expenses.

- **Considerations:** Policyholders should carefully evaluate the potential benefits and drawbacks before opting for a life settlement. The lump sum payment received may be less than the death benefit, and tax implications should be considered.

- **Regulation:** Life settlements are subject to regulatory oversight, and policyholders should work with reputable and licensed settlement providers.

4.4 Premium Taxations

The tax treatment of life insurance premiums and benefits varies based on the policy type and the jurisdiction's tax laws. Understanding the taxation of premiums is essential:

- **Premium Payments:** Premiums paid for personal life insurance coverage are generally not tax-deductible for individuals.

- **Death Benefit:** The death benefit received by beneficiaries upon the insured's passing is usually tax-free. However, in some cases, if the death benefit is paid in installments or includes interest, a portion may be subject to taxation.

- **Cash Value Growth:** The cash value growth within permanent life insurance policies is tax-deferred. This means that policyholders are only taxed on the cash value growth once they withdraw or surrender the policy.

- **Dividend Payments:** Dividends received from a participating whole life insurance policy are often considered a return of premium and are not subject to income tax.

It is important to consult with a tax advisor or financial professional to fully understand the tax implications of life insurance policies.

4.5 Beneficiaries

Beneficiaries are the individuals or entities designated by the policyholder to receive the death benefit upon the insured's passing. Selecting beneficiaries is a crucial decision that requires careful consideration. Key points about beneficiaries include:

- **Primary Beneficiaries:** Primary beneficiaries are the first to receive the death benefit. Policyholders can name one or more primary beneficiaries.

- **Contingent Beneficiaries:** Contingent beneficiaries are designated to receive the death benefit if the primary beneficiaries are no longer alive or unable to receive the benefit.

- **Revocable and Irrevocable Designations:** Beneficiary designations can be revocable or irrevocable. Revocable designations allow policyholders to change beneficiaries without consent, while irrevocable designations require the beneficiary's consent.

- **Per Stirpes and Per Capita:** These are methods used to distribute the death benefit among beneficiaries. Per stirpes distributes the benefit among branches of the family, while per capita distributes it equally among all beneficiaries.

Regularly reviewing and updating beneficiary designations is important, especially after major life events such as marriage, divorce, childbirth, or beneficiary passing.

4.6 Group Life Insurance

Employers or organizations typically offer group life insurance to cover a group of individuals. Key points about group life insurance include:

- **Coverage Amount:** Group policies often provide a predetermined amount of coverage, which may be based on the employee's salary or a fixed amount.

- **No Medical Underwriting:** Group policies typically do not require individuals to undergo medical exams or provide detailed medical history to qualify for coverage.

- **Portability:** Some group policies offer portability, allowing employees to convert their group coverage into an individual policy if they leave the group.

- **Premiums:** Premiums for group coverage may be lower than for individual policies by spreading the risk over a wider range of insured individuals.

Group life insurance can offer valuable coverage to employees and members of organizations, providing financial protection to their beneficiaries in the event of the insured's passing.

CHAPTER 5:
Policy Underwriting and Delivering

5.1 Contract Law

Health and life insurance contract law encompasses the legal principles, regulations, and rules that govern the formation, interpretation, and enforcement of contracts between insurance companies and policyholders for health and life insurance coverage. These laws are designed to protect the rights and interests of both parties and ensure that insurance contracts are fair, transparent, and enforceable. Here is an overview of key aspects of health and life insurance contract law:

1. Formation of the Contract:
   a. **Offer and Acceptance:** Like any contract, a health or life insurance contract requires an offer from the insurance company (contained in the policy) and the policyholder's acceptance (typically through paying premiums).

   b. **Legal Capacity:** Both parties must have the legal capacity to enter into a contract. They must be legally and mentally competent to understand and agree to the terms.

    c. **Consideration:** The policyholder pays premiums in exchange for the insurance company's promise to provide coverage.

2.   Contractual Terms and Disclosures:

    a. **Policy Provisions:** Insurance policies outline the terms and conditions of coverage, including benefits, exclusions, limitations, and obligations of both parties.

    b. **Duty of Good Faith and Fair Dealing:** Both parties must act in good faith and deal fairly in their interactions regarding the insurance contract.

    c. **Material Misrepresentations:** Policyholders must provide accurate and complete information during the application process. Material misrepresentations could lead to the denial of a claim or policy cancellation.

    d. **Disclosure of Policy Terms:** Insurance companies must disclose policy terms and conditions, including coverage limits, exclusions, and potential changes.

3.   Premium Payments:

    a. **Timely Payments:** Policyholders are responsible for paying premiums on time to keep the policy in force.

    b. **Grace Periods:** Insurance contracts often include a grace period that allows policyholders a certain amount of time (usually 30 days) to pay without the policy lapsing after a premium due date.

4.   Policyholder Rights and Remedies:

    a. **Right to Cancel:** Many health and life insurance contracts have a "free look" period during which the policyholder can review the contract and, if dissatisfied, cancel it for a full refund.

    b. **Claims Process:** Policyholders have the right to file claims for benefits and receive a fair and prompt claims process.

    c. **Dispute Resolution:** Insurance contracts often include dispute resolution provisions, such as arbitration or mediation.

5. Termination and Lapse:
    a. **Policy Termination:** Insurance contracts can be terminated by either party for various reasons, such as non-payment of premiums or the policyholder's request.

    b. **Lapse:** If premiums are not paid, the policy may lapse, resulting in a loss of coverage.

6. Regulatory Oversight:
    a. **State Insurance Departments:** Insurance contracts are subject to state laws and regulations. State insurance departments oversee insurance practices and ensure compliance with consumer protection laws.

    b. **Federal Laws:** Certain federal laws, such as the Affordable Care Act (ACA), impact health insurance contract requirements, including provisions related to pre-existing conditions, dependent coverage, and more.

7. Consumer Protections:
    a. **Unfair Practices:** Insurance contract law aims to prevent misleading or unfair practices by insurance companies, ensuring that policyholders are treated fairly.

    b. **Anti-Discrimination:** Health and life insurance contract law prohibits discrimination based on age, gender, race, or disability.

It is important for policyholders to thoroughly read and understand their insurance contracts, ask questions if needed, and seek legal or professional advice if they have concerns or disputes related to their coverage. Insurance contract law aims to create a balance between the interests of insurance companies and the protection of policyholders' rights.

5.2 Policy Underwriting

Underwriting a policy is a critical process that insurance companies use to evaluate and assess the risks associated with insuring an individual or entity. The underwriting process involves gathering and analyzing various factors to determine the insurance policy's terms, conditions, and premium rates. Whether it is for a life insurance policy, health insurance, property insurance, or any other type of coverage, underwriting helps insurance companies make informed decisions about insurability and pricing. Here is an overview of the underwriting process:

1. Application Submission: The process begins when the applicant (or entity seeking insurance) applies to the insurance company. The application provides essential information about the applicant's personal, health, financial, and other relevant details.

2. Information Collection: The insurance company collects a range of information to assess the risk associated with insuring the applicant. This may include:

- **Personal information:** Name, age, gender, address, occupation, and lifestyle factors.

- **Health history:** Medical conditions, medications, medical treatments, surgeries, and health habits.

- **Financial information:** Income, assets, liabilities, and other financial obligations.

- **Driving record (for auto insurance):** History of accidents, tickets, or violations.

- **Risk factors (for property insurance):** Location, type of property, safety features, and claims history.

- **Beneficiary and family information (for life insurance):** Details about beneficiaries and family members.

3. Underwriting Evaluation: During the evaluation process, the insurance company's underwriters analyze the gathered information to assess the risk of insuring the applicant. The goal is to determine the likelihood of a claim occurring and its potential severity. The evaluation helps the insurance company decide whether to offer coverage, the coverage limits, and the premium rate.

4. Risk Assessment: Underwriters use actuarial tables, statistical data, and predictive models to assess the risk associated with the applicant. They consider age, health status, occupation, lifestyle choices, and pre-existing conditions. The risk assessment helps the insurance company classify the applicant into risk categories.

5. Classifying Risk Categories: Underwriters assign the applicant to a risk category based on the risk assessment. Different risk categories correspond to different premium rates. For example, individuals with lower risk factors may receive preferred or standard rates, while those with higher risk factors may receive substandard rates.

6. Determining Terms and Premiums: The insurance company uses risk classification to determine the policy terms, including coverage limits, exclusions, and premium rates. Applicants with lower-risk classifications generally receive more favorable terms and lower premiums.

7. Decision Making: After completing the evaluation and risk assessment, the underwriter decides the applicant's insurability. The decision can include:

- **Acceptance:** The application is approved, and the insurance company offers coverage with specific terms and premium rates.

- **Decline:** The application is rejected due to high-risk factors or other reasons.

- **Counteroffer:** The insurance company may offer coverage with modified terms or at a different premium rate.

8. Communication with the Applicant: The insurance company communicates the underwriting decision to the applicant. If the application is approved, the applicant receives policy documents outlining the coverage, terms, conditions, and premium payment instructions.

9. Appeals and Further Information: Applicants who have declined coverage or receive less favorable terms may have the option to appeal the decision or provide additional information to support their application.

The underwriting process ensures that insurance companies accurately assess risk and offer appropriate coverage at fair premium rates. It helps balance the need to provide coverage with the financial viability of the insurance company. Applicants must provide accurate and complete information during the application process to ensure a thorough and accurate underwriting evaluation.

5.3 Application Completion

Completing an insurance application is a crucial step in obtaining insurance coverage, whether for life, health, property, or any other type of insurance. The information provided in the application forms the basis for the underwriting process and helps the insurance company assess the risk and determine the terms of coverage. Here is a comprehensive guide to completing an insurance application:

1. Obtain the Application Form: Obtain the appropriate application form from the insurance company, either physically or electronically. You may receive the form from an insurance agent, broker, or the insurance company's website.

2. Gather Necessary Information: Before starting the application, gather all the relevant information you will need to provide. This may include personal, health, financial, and other details.

3. Personal Information: Complete the sections that ask for your details, which may include:

- Full legal name
- Date of birth
- Gender
- Social Security number or other identification numbers
- Contact information (address, phone number, email)

4. Health Information: For health insurance or life insurance, provide accurate and detailed health-related information, such as:

- **Medical history:** Previous illnesses, surgeries, medications, treatments, hospitalizations, and chronic conditions.

- **Lifestyle choices:** Smoking, alcohol consumption, exercise habits, and any risky activities.

- **Family medical history:** Information about genetic health conditions within your family.

5. Financial Information: For some types of insurance, you may need to provide financial information, such as:

- Income and employment details
- Assets and liabilities
- Financial dependents

6. Coverage Details: Specify the type of coverage you are seeking, such as the coverage amount (for life insurance), the type of health insurance plan, or the property to be insured.

7. Beneficiary Designations: For life insurance, you must designate beneficiaries who will receive the death benefit. Provide their full names, relationships, and other required details.

8. Declarations and Signature: Review the application carefully, and ensure that all information is accurate and complete. Sign and date the application to certify the accuracy of the information. Your signature indicates your agreement to the terms and understanding of the information you provided.

9. Submission: Submit the completed application to the insurance company through the designated channel, including mailing a physical copy, submitting electronically through a secure online portal, or working with an insurance agent or broker.

10. Keep a Copy: Make a copy of the completed application for your records. This can be important for reference purposes and to verify the information you provided.

11. Follow-Up: You may need to contact an insurance provider to affirm receipt and inquire about your application's current state after submitting it.

12. Additional Information and Medical Exams: Depending on the type of insurance and the underwriting process, the insurance company may request additional information or medical examinations to assess your eligibility for coverage.

Tips for Completing the Application

- **Provide Accurate Information:** Accuracy is essential. Be truthful and thorough when providing information, as accurate or complete information could lead to coverage denials or complications in the future.

- **Seek Professional Guidance**: If you need clarification on any part of the application, consider seeking guidance from an insurance agent or broker.

- **Please review the Application:** Take your time to review the application before submitting it. Mistakes or omissions could affect the underwriting process.

- **Keep Copies:** Keep copies of all documents related to the application process for your records.

Completing an insurance application is a fundamental step in securing insurance coverage. By providing accurate and complete information, you will help ensure a smooth underwriting process and an accurate assessment of your coverage needs.

5.4 Policy Delivering

Delivering the insurance policy is the final step in obtaining insurance coverage. Once the underwriting process is complete and the application has been approved, the insurance company provides the policyholder with the official insurance policy document. Delivering the policy involves providing the policyholder with a physical or electronic copy of the policy, along with any necessary documentation and instructions. Here is what you need to know about delivering an insurance policy:

1. Notification of Approval: Once the insurance company has completed the underwriting process and approved the application, they will notify the policyholder of the approval and provide information about the next steps.

2. Policy Document Preparation: The insurance company prepares the policy document, which outlines the terms, conditions, coverage details, exclusions, premium payment schedule, and other important information related to the insurance coverage.

3. Delivery Options: Insurance policies can be delivered in various ways, depending on the insurance company's practices and the policyholder's preferences:

- **Physical Mail:** The policy document may be sent to the policyholder's mailing address through regular or certified mail.

- **Electronic Delivery:** Some insurance companies offer the option to receive policy documents electronically via email or through an online customer portal.

- **Agent or Broker:** If the policy was purchased through an insurance agent or broker, they may hand-deliver it to the policyholder or provide instructions for accessing it electronically.

4. Contents of the Policy: The insurance policy is a legally binding contract between the insurance company and the policyholder. It contains important information, such as:

- Policy number and effective date
- Coverage type and limits
- Premium payment details
- Beneficiary designations (for life insurance)
- Exclusions and limitations
- Claims procedures and contact information
- Termination and cancellation provisions
- Any additional riders or endorsements

5. Review and Verification: Upon receiving the policy, it is important for the policyholder to carefully review the document to ensure that all the information is accurate and matches their expectations. If there are any discrepancies or questions, the policyholder should contact the insurance company or their agent for clarification.

6. Safekeeping: The policyholder should keep the insurance policy safe and secure. Maintaining physical and electronic copies for reference and future claims processing is recommended.

7. Payment of Premiums: If premium payments are required, the policyholder should follow the premium payment schedule outlined in the policy. Pay premiums on time to avoid the policy lapsing or being canceled.

8. Contact Information: The policy document typically includes contact information for the insurance company's customer service, claims department, and other relevant departments. This information should be saved for future reference.

9. Changes and Updates: If changes to the policyholder's circumstances or updates are needed (such as changing beneficiaries or updating contact information), the policyholder should promptly notify the insurance company.

Delivering the policy marks the completion of the insurance application process and the beginning of the coverage period. Policyholders should keep their insurance policy in a secure and easily accessible place, review its contents periodically, and contact the insurance company or their agent if they have any questions or need assistance.

5.5 Anti-Money Laundering

Life insurance companies play a significant role in anti-money laundering (AML) efforts to prevent the abuse of their services for illegal financial activities. AML measures within the life insurance industry aim to detect and deter money laundering, financial crimes, and terrorist financing. Here is an overview of how life insurance companies address AML:

1. Customer Due Diligence (CDD) and Know Your Customer (KYC): Life insurance companies must conduct thorough customer due diligence to verify the identity of policyholders and beneficiaries. This involves collecting and verifying personal information, such as name, address, date of birth, and source of funds. Enhanced due diligence can be applied to high-risk customers such as politically exposed persons or those from higher-risk jurisdictions.

2. Risk Assessment: Life insurance companies assess the risks associated with their customers and policies. A risk-based approach helps identify high-risk transactions, products, or customers that may require additional scrutiny and monitoring.

3. Suspicious Activity Reporting (SAR): Life insurance companies monitor transactions for unusual or suspicious activity that may indicate illicit activities or money laundering. When suspicious activity is identified, they file Suspicious Activity Reports (SARs) with relevant authorities as required by law.

4. Training and Awareness: Employees of life insurance companies receive training on recognizing and reporting suspicious activities. Training ensures staff members know AML requirements and their responsibilities in preventing money laundering.

5. Policies and Procedures: Life insurance companies establish comprehensive AML policies and procedures that outline how AML measures are implemented across the organization. These policies include guidelines for customer onboarding, transaction monitoring, reporting, and risk assessment.

6. Beneficial Ownership Disclosure: Life insurance companies may require policyholders to disclose information about beneficial owners, particularly in cases where policies are purchased through trusts or other legal entities.

7. Sanctions Screening: Life insurance companies screen customers and transactions against sanctions lists to ensure they are not providing insurance coverage to individuals or entities subject to economic sanctions.

8. Technology and Data Analytics: Life insurance companies leverage advanced technology and data analytics to monitor transactions and detect patterns of suspicious activity. Automated systems help identify unusual behavior and trigger alerts for further investigation.

9. Collaboration with Authorities: Life insurance companies collaborate with regulatory and law enforcement agencies to share information, report suspicious activities, and contribute to broader AML efforts.

10. Anti-Fraud Measures: AML efforts often overlap with anti-fraud measures, which involve identifying and preventing illicit financial activities. Life insurance companies implement fraud detection and prevention measures to safeguard against fraudulent insurance claims and policyholder activities.

11. Regulatory Compliance: government agencies and regulatory bodies subject to AML regulations and requirements establish life insurance companies. Non-compliance can lead to penalties, fines, and reputational damage.

12. Ongoing Monitoring: AML efforts are ongoing, and life insurance companies continuously monitor transactions and customer behavior to detect and prevent potential risks.

Anti-money laundering measures within the life insurance industry are essential for maintaining the financial system's integrity, protecting policyholders, and contributing to broader global AML efforts. By adhering to strict AML procedures, life insurance companies play a critical role in preventing financial crimes and ensuring the legitimate use of their services.

5.6 Replacement

Life insurance replacement refers to canceling an existing life insurance policy and purchasing a new one. This can occur when a policyholder switches from one life insurance policy to another within the same insurance company or with a different one. While replacement can be a legitimate and beneficial decision under certain circumstances, it is important to carefully evaluate its reasons and consider potential implications. Here is a comprehensive look at life insurance replacement:

Reasons for Life Insurance Replacement

1. **Better Terms and Rates:** Policyholders may seek a replacement if they find a new policy that offers terms that are more favorable, higher coverage, or lower premiums.

2. **Change in Needs:** Life circumstances, such as marriage, the birth of a child, or increased financial responsibilities, may lead to a need for different coverage.

3. **Improved Features:** Newer policies may include additional features like riders or benefits that suit better the policyholder's goals.

4. **Investment Opportunities:** Some policies offer cash value accumulation or investment components, and policyholders may opt for a replacement to access potentially higher returns.

Key Considerations for Replacement

1. **Costs:** Replacement often involves new underwriting, which means the policyholder may need to pay application fees, undergo a medical examination, and potentially face higher premiums if health conditions have changed.

2. **Waiting Periods:** If a new policy is purchased, there may be waiting periods before certain benefits, such as the full death benefit, become effective.

3. **Loss of Benefits:** Existing policies may have benefits that would be forfeited upon replacement, such as waiting periods for specific coverage or accumulated cash value.

4. **Tax Implications:** Surrendering an existing policy could lead to taxable events, particularly if there is a gain in cash value. It is essential to understand potential tax consequences.

5. **Health Changes:** If the policyholder's health has deteriorated since the original policy was issued, obtaining a new policy could result in higher premiums or even policy denial.

Replacement Regulations and Protections

Given the potential risks and consequences of replacement, insurance regulators have established guidelines to protect consumers:

1. **Replacement Regulations:** Many jurisdictions require insurers and agents to follow specific procedures when replacing a policy. This often includes providing policyholders with a "Notice Regarding Replacement" that explains the consequences of replacement.

2. **Free Look Period:** Many insurance policies, including replacement policies, have a "free look" period during which the policyholder can review the new policy and cancel it for a full refund if dissatisfied.

3. **Disclosure:** Insurance professionals must provide accurate and complete information about existing and proposed new policies to help the policyholder make an informed decision.

Guidelines for Evaluating Replacement

1. **Needs Analysis:** Assess whether the new policy meets your current and future financial needs. Consider factors like coverage amount, beneficiaries, and any specific goals.

2. **Comparison:** Thoroughly compare the features, benefits, costs, and terms of the existing and new policies.

3. **Existing Policy Review:** Evaluate your current policy to understand any benefits or features that could be lost upon replacement.

4. **Health Considerations:** If your health has changed, consider the impact on insurability and premium rates.

5. **Financial Impact:** Understand the costs associated with replacement, including potential surrender charges and tax implications.

6. **Professional Advice:** Contact a qualified financial advisor or insurance professional who can provide guidance tailored to your situation.

Life insurance replacement can be viable when it aligns with your changing needs and goals. However, careful evaluation, understanding the potential risks and consequences, and seeking professional guidance is essential to ensure that replacement is the right choice for you.

5.7 Exclusions

Life insurance exclusions are specific circumstances, events, or situations not covered by a life insurance policy. Exclusions define coverage limits and outline scenarios where the insurance company will not pay the death benefit to the policy's beneficiaries. Policyholders need to understand these exclusions before purchasing a life insurance policy to ensure they clearly understand the coverage provided. Here are some common life insurance exclusions:

1. Suicide Clause: Suicide clauses are common in life insurance policies, typically within the first two years of the policy. If the insured commits suicide during this period, the insurance company may not pay the full death benefit. Instead, the insurance company could reimburse the premiums or offer a limited reimbursement. After the clause's expiration, suicides are typically covered.

2. Contestability Period: Within the contestability period, which is typically among the first & second years of the policy, the insurance provider has the right to investigate and potentially deny a claim based on a policyholder's lies and concealment of important information.

3. Material Misrepresentation: If the policyholder provides false or incomplete information on the application that would have affected the underwriting process or the insurer's decision to issue the policy, the insurance company may deny a claim.

4. High-Risk Activities: Certain high-risk activities, such as extreme sports, aviation, or dangerous hobbies, may be excluded from coverage. The policy might not pay the death benefit if the insured dies while engaging in these activities.

5. Acts of War or Terrorism: Some policies exclude coverage for deaths resulting from acts of war, terrorism, or military service during the conflict.

6. Illegal Activities: The policy may not pay the death benefit if the insured dies while engaged in illegal activities.

7. Specific Health Conditions or Activities: Certain health conditions or activities might be excluded from coverage, especially if not disclosed during underwriting. Examples include hazardous occupations, drug or alcohol abuse, or undisclosed pre-existing health conditions.

8. Non-Payment of Premiums: If the policy lapses due to non-payment of premiums, the death benefit may not be paid. However, some policies have grace periods during which the policy can be reinstated.

9. Non-Accidental Death: Some policies exclude coverage for deaths that are not accidental, such as illness, natural causes, or medical complications.

10. Specific Exclusions or Riders: Certain policy exclusions may be specific to the terms of the policy or related riders. For example, a life insurance policy with an accidental death rider might exclude deaths from non-accidental causes.

11. Aviation or Hazardous Activities: If the insured regularly participates in aviation, skydiving, or other hazardous activities, the policy may have exclusions related to these activities.

It is crucial for policyholders to carefully review the terms and conditions of a life insurance policy, including any exclusions, before purchasing coverage. If there are concerns about specific exclusions, policyholders can discuss them with an insurance agent or company representative to understand the impact on coverage. Being fully aware of exclusions ensures that the policyholder and beneficiaries clearly understand the circumstances under which the death benefit may not be paid.

CHAPTER 6:
Health Insurance Policy Types

Health insurance is a vital tool that provides individuals and families access to necessary medical care while offering financial protection against healthcare expenses. Different types of health insurance policies cater to varying needs and preferences. This chapter will explore various health insurance options, including accidental and health insurance, disability coverage, accidental death insurance, long-term care insurance, medical expense insurance, managed care plans (HMO, PPO, and POS), hospital indemnity insurance, and group insurance.

6.1 Accidental and Health Insurance Basics

Accidental and health insurance policies are designed to cover medical expenses, accidents, injuries, and illnesses. These policies offer financial protection against unforeseen events and help individuals and families manage unexpected healthcare costs. Key aspects of accidental and health insurance policies include:

- **Coverage Scope:** Accidental and health insurance policies cover various medical expenses, including hospitalizations, surgeries, doctor visits, prescription medications, and emergency care.

- **Accidental Injuries:** These policies typically cover injuries resulting from accidents, such as fractures, burns, dislocations, and other accidental injuries.

- **Illness Coverage:** Besides accidental injuries, many policies cover illnesses and medical conditions, ensuring comprehensive protection for various health-related events.

- **Lump Sum Benefit:** In case of a covered accident or illness, the policyholder or beneficiary may receive a lump sum payment. This payment can cover medical expenses, rehabilitation, or other financial needs.

- **Critical Illness Coverage:** Some accidental and health insurance policies offer coverage for specific critical illnesses, such as cancer, heart attack, stroke, and kidney failure.

- **Waiting Periods:** Policies may include waiting periods before certain benefits become effective. It is important to understand the waiting period and coverage limitations outlined in the policy.

- **Pre-Existing Conditions:** Policies may have exclusions or limitations related to pre-existing conditions. Reviewing the policy details helps clarify how pre-existing conditions are addressed.

6.2 Option for Disability

Disability insurance is a vital form of coverage that offers income replacement in the event of a covered disability that prevents an individual from working. This type of insurance provides financial support during periods of disability, ensuring that individuals can meet their financial obligations. Key features of disability insurance include:

- **Income Replacement:** Disability insurance replaces a percentage of the policyholder's income if they cannot work due to a covered disability. The benefit amount is typically based on the individual's pre-disability earnings.

- **Short-Term and Long-Term Disability:** Disability insurance can be categorized into short-term and long-term coverage. Short-term disability policies provide benefits for a limited duration, often several months. Long-term disability policies offer benefits for a more extended period, possibly until retirement age.

- **Definition of Disability:** The policy specifies the definition of disability, which determines when an individual is considered disabled and eligible for benefits. Definitions may include the inability to perform one's occupation or any suitable occupation based on education and experience.

- **Waiting Period:** Disability insurance policies have a waiting period, also known as an elimination period, which is the period between the onset of disability and the start of benefit payments. A longer waiting period can lead to lower premiums.

- **Partial Disability:** Some policies cover partial disability, where the policyholder can still work but experiences a reduced income due to the disability.

- **Own-Occupation vs. Any-Occupation:** Disability policies may define disability based on the individual's ability to perform their occupation (own-occupation policy) or any occupation for which they are reasonably suited (any-occupation policy).

6.3 Medical Expense Insurance

Medical expense insurance, or hospitalization insurance, covers hospital stays, medical treatments, surgeries, and other healthcare services. This type of insurance helps individuals and families manage the costs of medical care and ensures they have access to necessary treatments. Key aspects of medical expense insurance include:

- **Coverage Scope:** Medical expense insurance covers various medical services and treatments, including hospitalizations, surgeries, doctor visits, diagnostic tests, prescription medications, and emergency care.

- **Hospitalization Benefits:** These policies often provide specific benefits for hospital stays, including coverage for room and board, surgical procedures, and related medical expenses.

- **Outpatient Services:** Medical expense insurance may cover outpatient services such as consultations with specialists, diagnostic procedures, and outpatient surgeries.

- **Network Coverage:** Some medical expense insurance plans require members to use a network of healthcare providers to receive coverage. Out-of-network care may have higher costs or may not be covered.

- **Deductibles and Copayments:** Policies typically involve deductibles and copayments, where the policyholder is responsible for a portion of the healthcare costs. Higher deductibles and copayments may result in lower premiums.

- **Prescription Drug Coverage:** Many medical expense insurance policies include protection for prescription medications as part of the base policy or through optional riders.

- **Preventive Care:** Vaccinations, screenings, and regular health examinations are preventive care your policy may cover.

6.4 Long-Term Care Insurance

Long-term care insurance addresses the costs associated with long-term care services, such as nursing home care, assisted living, and home healthcare. This coverage helps individuals plan for future healthcare needs and ensures they have the financial means to receive necessary care. Key features of long-term care insurance include:

- **Long-Term Care Coverage:** People who have difficulty conducting tasks related to daily living (ADLs) on their own are eligible for services covered by long-term care insurance. These services may include bathing, dressing, feeding, transferring, toileting, & continence assistance.

- **Settings of Care:** Long-term care insurance covers various settings, including nursing homes, assisted living facilities, adult day care centers, and home healthcare.

- **Benefit Amount and Duration:** Policies specify the maximum benefit amount and duration of coverage. Some policies have a lifetime maximum benefit, while others offer benefits for a specific number of years.

- **Waiting Period (Elimination Period):** Long-term care insurance policies often have a waiting period, which is the period between when the individual becomes eligible for benefits and when the coverage starts. The length of the waiting period affects the policy's cost.

- **Inflation Protection:** Some policies offer inflation protection options to account for rising healthcare costs over time.

- **Hybrid Policies:** Hybrid policies combine LTCi with another type of insurance, such as life or annuity coverage. If healthcare benefits are not needed, these insurance payouts either upon death or as an annuity.

6.5 Accidental Death Insurance

Accidental death insurance is a specialized form of coverage that benefits the beneficiary in the event of the death of the insured caused by an accident. This type of insurance focuses on offering financial support specifically for accidental fatalities. Key aspects of accidental death insurance include:

- **Coverage Focus:** Accidental death insurance addresses accidental deaths and does not cover deaths resulting from natural causes or illnesses.

- **Lump Sum Benefit:** If the insured dies due to an accident covered by the policy, the beneficiary receives a lump sum payment. This payment can help cover funeral expenses, outstanding debts, or other financial needs.

- **Exclusions:** Accidental death insurance policies may include specific exclusions, such as deaths resulting from drug overdoses, self-inflicted injuries, or activities not covered by the policy.

- **Additional Riders:** Some policies offer additional riders or options that extend coverage to include specific events, such as accidental dismemberment or common carrier accidents (e.g., plane crashes).

- **No Medical Exam:** Accidental death insurance policies often do not require a medical exam for underwriting, making it relatively straightforward to obtain coverage.

- **Affordability:** Accidental death insurance is generally more affordable than comprehensive life insurance policies because it covers a specific event type.

6.6 PPO, HMO, and POS Plans

Managed care plans, including Preferred Provider Organization (PPO), Health Maintenance Organization (HMO), and Point of Service (POS) plans, offer different approaches to accessing healthcare services and managing costs. These plans often involve a network of healthcare providers and specific rules for obtaining care. Key features of each plan type include:

- **Health Maintenance Organization (HMO) Plans:**

  o Members select a primary care physician (PCP) from the network.

  o Referrals from the PCP are typically required to see specialists.

  o Coverage is generally limited to in-network providers.

  o HMOs emphasize preventive care and coordination of healthcare services.

  o Lower out-of-pocket costs are common within the network.

- **Preferred Provider Organization (PPO) Plans:**

  o Members have more flexibility in choosing healthcare providers.

  o Referrals are optional to see specialists.

  o Both in-network and out-of-network care are covered, though out-of-network care is usually more expensive.

  o PPO plans offer greater autonomy in managing healthcare decisions.

- **Point of Service (POS) Plans:**

  o POS plans to combine features of HMO and PPO plans.

  o Members choose a primary care physician but can see out-of-network providers with referrals.

  o In-network care is generally more cost-effective.

  o POS plans provide flexibility while maintaining some aspects of care coordination.

6.7 Group Insurance

Group health insurance is a type of coverage offered by employers or organizations to provide healthcare benefits to individuals. This form of insurance often offers cost savings, broader coverage, and easier eligibility than individual policies. Key features of group insurance include:

- **Employer-Sponsored Coverage:** Many employers offer group health insurance as part of their employee benefits package, allowing employees to access healthcare coverage at a group rate.

- **Cost Sharing:** Group insurance typically involves cost sharing between the employer and employees, with employers often subsidizing a portion of the premiums.

- **Broader Coverage:** Group plans often provide comprehensive coverage that includes hospitalizations, doctor visits, prescription medications, preventive care, and more.

- **Easier Eligibility:** Group insurance may have less stringent underwriting requirements than individual policies, making it easier for employees to obtain coverage.

- **Premium Stability:** Group insurance premiums are often more stable and predictable than individual policies, as the risk is spread across a larger pool of individuals.

- **Family Coverage:** Group insurance allows employees to extend coverage to their family members, offering a convenient way to provide healthcare benefits for dependents.

6.8 Hospital Indemnity Insurance

Hospital indemnity insurance provides a fixed cash benefit for each day an individual is hospitalized due to a covered illness or injury. This type of insurance helps individuals manage the costs associated with hospital stays and related expenses. Key features of hospital indemnity insurance include:

- **Cash Benefit:** Hospital indemnity insurance provides a predetermined cash benefit for each day spent in the hospital due to a covered event.

- **Coverage for Hospitalization:** This insurance type focuses on hospital stays and may not cover outpatient care, doctor visits, or other medical services.

- **Supplemental Coverage:** Hospital indemnity insurance is often used to supplement other health insurance coverage and help cover out-of-pocket expenses.

- **No Network Restrictions:** Policyholders can use the cash benefit as needed, regardless of whether they receive care from in-network or out-of-network providers.

- **Coverage Flexibility:** Individuals can choose the daily benefit amount and coverage duration based on their needs and budget.

CHAPTER 7:
Health Policy Provisions, Riders and Clauses

7.1 Mandatory Provisions

Mandatory provisions in a health insurance policy are legal requirements that must be included to ensure that policyholders are adequately protected and that their rights are upheld. These provisions are typically mandated by state insurance laws or regulations and establish certain rights and responsibilities for the insurance company and the policyholder. Here are some of the key mandatory provisions that are commonly found in health insurance policies:

1. Entire Contract: This provision states that the policy and any attached riders or endorsements constitute the entire contract between the insurance company and the policyholder. It ensures that all the terms and conditions of the insurance arrangement are clearly outlined in the policy.

2. Grace Period: The grace period provision allows the policyholder a period (usually 30 days) after the premium due date to make premium payments without the risk of policy termination. Coverage remains in force during the grace period, providing a buffer for late payments.

3. Incontestability: After a certain period (often two years) from the policy's effective date, the incontestability provision prevents the insurance company from contesting or voiding the policy due to material misstatements or omissions on the application. This provision promotes stability and prevents policies from being retroactively challenged.

4. Policy Renewal: This provision outlines the terms under which the policy can be renewed or continued. It specifies the conditions that may lead to non-renewal, cancellation, or termination of the policy.

5. Termination: The termination provision describes the circumstances under which the insurance company or the policyholder may terminate the policy. It often includes procedures and notice requirements for termination.

6. Conversion Privilege: For group health insurance policies, the conversion privilege provision allows an insured individual whose coverage ends to convert to an individual policy without evidence of insurability (proof of good health). This provision ensures continued coverage for individuals leaving a group plan.

7. Continuation or Conversion Rights: Similar to the conversion privilege, this provision allows an insured individual whose coverage is ending (e.g., due to job loss) to continue or convert it to an individual policy.

8. Limitations and Exclusions: The policy must clearly outline the limitations and exclusions of coverage. This includes specifying what is not covered by the policy, such as pre-existing conditions or specific treatments.

9. Proof of Loss: The proof of loss provision establishes the process and timeframe for submitting a claim to the insurance company. It outlines the documentation required to support a claim and the procedures for filing it.

10. Notice of Claim: This provision outlines the policyholder's obligation to notify the insurance company of a claim within a specified timeframe after a covered event or loss.

11. Claim Settlement: The claim settlement provision details the procedures and timeframes for the insurance company to review, process, and settle a claim. It ensures that claims are handled promptly and fairly.

12. Payment of Claims: This provision specifies how and when the insurance company will make claim payments to the policyholder or the medical provider. It includes information on the method of payment and any applicable timelines.

13. Other Insurance: The other insurance provision clarifies how the policy coordinates with other insurance coverage the policyholder may have. It addresses how benefits will be coordinated when multiple insurance policies are in effect.

14. Conformity with State Laws: Conformity with state laws provision ensures that the policy complies with the state's insurance laws and regulations.

15. Fraud: The fraud provision states that the policy will be void if the policyholder, with intent to defraud, submits false information or makes false statements concerning the policy.

These mandatory provisions help create a standardized framework for health insurance policies, ensuring that policyholders are informed about their rights, responsibilities, and terms of coverage. Policyholders need to review and understand these provisions when purchasing a health insurance policy to ensure they clearly understand their coverage and obligations.

7.2 Right of Renewability

The "Right of Renewability" is a crucial provision in health insurance policies that outlines the policyholder's entitlement to renew their health insurance coverage. This provision ensures that individuals who have purchased a health insurance policy can continue their coverage beyond the initial policy term, subject to certain conditions. The right of renewability is intended to provide policyholders with ongoing access to healthcare coverage and protection, especially in times of need. Here is an overview of the key aspects of the right of renewability in health insurance policies:

1. Guaranteed Renewability: Many health insurance policies offer guaranteed renewability, particularly individual and group health plans. This means that the insurance company is obligated to renew the policy for the policyholder as long as the policyholder continues to pay the premiums and complies with the policy terms. Guaranteed renewability ensures that policyholders can maintain continuous coverage without the risk of non-renewal or cancellation due to changes in their health status.

2. Premium Adjustments: While the insurance company is generally required to renew the policy, they may adjust the premium rates upon renewal. Premium adjustments are typically based on factors such as the policyholder's age, location, claims history, and changes in the overall risk pool. Premium increases are subject to state insurance regulations and guidelines.

3. Renewal Period: The renewal period refers to when the policyholder can renew their health insurance coverage. The length of the renewal period can vary depending on the type of policy and the insurance company. Policyholders must be aware of the renewal period and submit their application within the specified timeframe.

4. Continuation of Benefits: The right of renewability ensures that the benefits and coverage under the policy remain consistent upon renewal. Policyholders can generally expect to maintain the same level of coverage for essential healthcare services, subject to any changes outlined in the policy.

5. Pre-Existing Conditions: Health insurance policies with guaranteed renewability often cannot exclude coverage for pre-existing conditions upon renewal. If a policyholder develops a medical condition during the policy term, the insurance company cannot use that condition as a basis for denying or limiting coverage upon renewal.

6. Policy Changes: While the benefits and coverage typically remain consistent upon renewal, insurance companies may change other policy aspects, such as the premium rates, deductible amounts, or co-payment structure. Policyholders should review renewal notices carefully to understand any changes that may apply.

7. Timely Premium Payments: To maintain the right of renewability, policyholders must ensure timely payment of their premium premiums. Failure to pay premiums within the grace period (if applicable) may terminate the policy.

8. State Regulations and Exceptions: State insurance regulations and laws may influence the specific details of the right of renewability provision. Some policies may have exceptions or limitations based on state laws, and policies provided by certain organizations (such as employer-sponsored plans) may have different renewal provisions.

9. Continuous Coverage: The right of renewability is vital in promoting continuous health insurance coverage. By allowing policyholders to renew their policies, even if they have experienced health issues, the provision helps prevent coverage gaps and ensures that individuals have access to medical care when needed.

It is important for individuals considering health insurance coverage to thoroughly review the terms and conditions of the right of renewability provision. This provision offers valuable protection and peace of mind, as it guarantees the option to maintain coverage over time, regardless of changes in health status. Policyholders should consult with their insurance agent or company representative to fully understand the implications of the right of renewability in their specific health insurance policy.

7.3 Riders

Health insurance riders are additional provisions or benefits that can be added to a basic health insurance policy to enhance coverage and tailor the policy to meet specific needs. These riders allow policyholders to customize their health insurance coverage by adding specific benefits or features beyond what is offered in the standard policy. Riders are a way to address unique healthcare needs and preferences, allowing individuals to create a more comprehensive and personalized insurance plan. Here are some common health insurance riders that policyholders may consider:

1. Critical Illness Rider: This rider provides a flat sum benefit if the insured gets diagnosed with a critical illness, like cancer, a heart attack, kidney failure, or a stroke. The benefit can be used to pay for medical expenses, treatments, and other expenses that may arise due to the illness.

2. Accident Benefit Rider: An accident benefit rider offers an additional payout if the insured sustains injuries due to an accident. It can help cover medical, rehabilitation, and other accident-related expenses.

3. Hospital Cash Rider: With this rider, the insured receives a daily cash benefit for each day spent in the hospital due to illness or injury. The cash benefit can help offset additional costs associated with hospitalization.

4. Surgical Expense Rider: This rider covers surgical procedures, including surgeon's fees, anesthesia, operating room costs, and related expenses. It ensures that the insured has financial support for surgical treatments.

5. Maternity Rider: A maternity rider covers pregnancy-related medical expenses, including prenatal care, childbirth, and postnatal care. It may cover hospitalization, doctor visits, and other maternity-related services.

6. Prescription Drug Rider: This rider provides coverage for prescription medications beyond what is included in the standard health insurance policy. It helps reduce out-of-pocket costs for prescription drugs.

7. Dental and Vision Rider: A dental and vision rider extends coverage to dental and vision care services, such as routine check-ups, cleanings, eyeglasses, and contact lenses.

8. Home Healthcare Rider: With this rider, the insured can receive coverage for home healthcare services, such as nursing care, physical therapy, and medical equipment, if they require care at home due to illness or injury.

9. Wellness and Preventive Care Rider: This rider covers the costs of wellness visits, preventive screenings, vaccinations, and other preventive healthcare services to encourage proactive health management.

10. Out-of-network Rider: An out-of-network rider provides coverage for medical services obtained from healthcare providers not part of the insurance company's network. It helps reduce the financial impact of using out-of-network providers.

11. Long-Term Care Rider: This rider extends coverage to long-term care services, such as nursing home care and assisted living. It helps policyholders cover the costs of extended care due to age or disability.

12. Rehabilitation Rider: A rehabilitation rider offers coverage for rehabilitation services, including physical therapy, occupational therapy, and speech therapy, following an injury or illness.

13. Second Medical Opinion Rider: This rider provides coverage for seeking a second opinion before undergoing a significant medical procedure or treatment.

14. Travel Medical Rider: For individuals who travel frequently, a travel medical rider offers coverage for medical expenses incurred while abroad.

It is important for policyholders to carefully review the terms, coverage limits, and costs associated with each rider before adding them to their health insurance policy. Riders can significantly enhance coverage, but they also affect premium costs. Consulting with an insurance agent or representative can help individuals decide which riders are most suitable for their healthcare needs and budget.

7.4 Clauses

Health insurance policies include various clauses that outline the terms, conditions, and coverage provisions. These clauses define the rights and responsibilities of both the policyholder and the insurance company. Policyholders must understand these clauses to make informed decisions about their coverage. Here are some important health insurance policy clauses:

1. Definitions Clause: This clause provides definitions for key terms and terms used throughout the policy. It ensures clarity and a common understanding of the terminology used in the policy.

2. Insuring Clause: The insuring clause states the policy's scope of coverage. It outlines the types of medical expenses or services covered by the policy.

3. Exclusions Clause: Exclusions are specific situations, conditions, or treatments not covered by the policy. This clause outlines the circumstances under which the insurance company will not provide coverage.

4. Limitations Clause: The limitations clause outlines any restrictions on coverage, such as limits on the number of visits or treatment services.

5. Pre-Existing Condition Clause: This clause addresses coverage for pre-existing medical conditions. It explains how the policy treats conditions before the policy is purchased.

6. Waiting Period Clause: The waiting period clause specifies the period that must pass before certain benefits become effective. For example, a policy might have a waiting period for coverage of specific treatments.

7. Coordination of Benefits Clause: This clause applies when insured individuals have coverage under multiple health insurance policies. It explains how benefits will be coordinated between different insurance plans to prevent overpayment.

8. Grace Period Clause: The grace period clause allows the policyholder a specific timeframe (usually 30 days) to make payment without losing coverage after the premium due date. During this period, coverage remains in force.

9. Renewability Clause: This clause outlines the policyholder's right to renew the policy when it expires, subject to certain conditions. It provides details about premium adjustments, terms of renewal, and any changes that may apply.

10. Termination Clause: The termination clause explains the circumstances under which the insurance company or the policyholder can terminate the policy. It may outline the procedures and notice requirements for termination.

11. Claim Filing and Settlement Clause: This clause details the procedures and timeframes for filing claims, as well as the process for the insurance company to review, process, and settle claims.

12. Incontestability Clause: After a specified period (usually two years), the incontestability clause prevents the insurance company from contesting or voiding the policy based on misstatements or omissions on the application.

13. Conversion Clause: In-group health insurance, the conversion clause allows an insured individual to convert their group policy to an individual policy if they leave the group or lose eligibility.

14. Continuation or Portability Clause: Similar to the conversion clause, this provision allows insured individual to continue their coverage under the same policy, even if they leave the group or employer.

15. Subrogation Clause: The subrogation clause gives the insurance company the right to recover payment from a third party if the insured person receives compensation for medical expenses from that party.

16. Assignment Clause: This clause outlines the conditions under which the policyholder can transfer their rights or benefits under the policy to another person or entity.

17. Change of Policy Terms Clause: This clause explains how changes to the policy terms and conditions may occur and how the insurance company will notify the policyholder of such changes.

18. Notice of Claim Clause: This clause outlines the policyholder's responsibility to notify the insurance company promptly when a claim arises and specifies the information required for claims processing.

19. Premium Payment Clause: This clause outlines the policyholder's obligation to pay premiums, including due dates, grace periods, and consequences of non-payment.

20. Conformity with State Laws Clause: This clause ensures the policy complies with state insurance laws and regulations.

It is important for policyholders to thoroughly review these clauses and any other provisions in their health insurance policy. If there are any uncertainties or questions about the policy terms, seeking clarification from the insurance company or a qualified professional is recommended. Understanding the clauses helps policyholders make informed decisions and effectively utilize their health insurance coverage when needed.

CHAPTER 8:
Social Insurance

S ocial insurance programs provide financial Security and healthcare access to individuals and families in various countries. These programs are designed to address specific populations' economic and healthcare needs, often focusing on retirees, disabled individuals, and those with limited financial resources. This chapter will explore two significant social insurance programs: Social Security benefits and Medicare.

8.1 Benefits of Social Security

Social Security is a comprehensive social insurance plan established in the United States to provide financial support to eligible individuals and families during retirement, disability, or other life events. The program operates as a social safety net, helping to prevent poverty and ensuring a basic income level for retirees and disabled individuals. Social security benefits are financed through payroll taxes and fees provide a foundation of economic stability for millions of Americans.

Key Aspects of Social Security Benefits

1. Retirement Benefits: Social Security retirement benefits provide a source of income to eligible individuals who have reached the designated retirement age (currently 62 to 67, depending on birth year). The benefit amount is based on the individual's work history and earnings.

2. Disability Benefits: Social Security disability benefits are available to individuals with a qualifying disability that prevents them from carrying out a remunerative activity. Applicants must meet specific medical and work history criteria to be eligible for disability benefits.

3. Survivor Benefits: Survivor benefits provide financial support to the surviving spouse, children, or other eligible dependents of a deceased worker eligible for Social Security benefits. These benefits help ensure financial stability for families facing the loss of a breadwinner.

4. Cost-of-Living Adjustments (COLA): Social Security benefits are adjusted annually based on changes in the cost of living to help beneficiaries keep up with inflation.

5. Medicare Enrollment: Most individuals who qualify for Social Security benefits are also eligible for Medicare, the government-funded health insurance program for seniors and certain disabled individuals.

6. Earnings Record: Social Security benefits are determined based on an individual's earnings record, which reflects their lifetime earnings subject to Social Security payroll taxes.

7. Full Retirement Age (FRA): The full retirement age is when individuals can receive their full Social Security retirement benefit. It is based on the individual's birth year and is important in determining benefit amounts.

8. Early Retirement: While individuals can start receiving Social Security benefits as early as 62, opting for early retirement results in reduced benefits compared to waiting until full retirement age.

9. Delayed Retirement Credits: Individuals who delay claiming Social Security benefits beyond their full retirement age can receive increased monthly benefits, known as delayed retirement credits.

10. Benefit Calculation: The Social Security Administration uses a formula to calculate benefits based on the average indexed monthly earnings during the highest-earning years.

8.2 Medicare

Medicare is a federal health insurance plan in the United States; it provides insurance coverage to persons aged 65 years and older and also to some disabled persons. The program is designed to ensure access to essential healthcare services and reduce financial burdens associated with medical expenses.

Key Aspects of Medicare

1. Medicare Part A: Hospital Insurance encompasses hospitalizations, care in skilled nursing facilities, hospice care, and home health services. Most people enroll in Part A of the program when they become eligible for benefits from Social Security.

2. Medicare Part B: Medical Insurance includes coverage for ambulatory services, doctor visits, preventative care, and specific medical supplies. Part B coverage is subject to a monthly premium paid by beneficiaries.

3. Medicare Part C: Medicare Advantage is offered by private insurance companies and provides all the benefits of Part A and Part B, along with additional benefits such as vision, dental, and prescription drug coverage.

4. Medicare Part D: Prescription Drug Coverage provides coverage for prescription drugs through private insurance programs. Beneficiaries can enroll in either a Medicare Part D stand-alone plan or an Advantage plan for Medicare with coverage for prescription drugs.

5. Medicare Supplement Insurance: Medigap policies have private insurance plans that help cover Medicare-excluded out-of-pocket expenses, such as copayments, deductibles, & coinsurance.

6. Enrollment Periods: Initial enrollment for Medicare typically begins three months before an individual turns 65 and continues for seven months (three months before, the month of, and three months after the 65th birthday).

7. Special Enrollment Periods: Certain circumstances, such as working past age 65 with employer-based coverage, may qualify individuals for special enrollment periods without penalties.

8. Preventive Services: Medicare covers a range of preventive services, screenings, and vaccines to help beneficiaries maintain their health and catch potential issues early.

9. Coverage for Certain Disabilities: Individuals under 65 receiving Social Security disability benefits for at least 24 months are eligible for Medicare coverage.

10. Medicare Savings Programs: These programs provide financial assistance to eligible individuals with limited income and resources, helping them pay for Medicare premiums, deductibles, and coinsurance.

11. Part A and Part B Premiums: Most beneficiaries do not pay a premium for Part A if they or their spouse has paid Medicare taxes for a specified period. Part B premiums are income-dependent.

12. Medicare for All and Healthcare Reform: There have been ongoing discussions and proposals for healthcare reform, including "Medicare for All," which aims to expand access to healthcare coverage to all Americans through a single-payer system.

In conclusion, Social Security benefits and Medicare are integral components of the social insurance framework in the United States. Social Security provides financial support during retirement, disability, and to survivors, while Medicare offers essential health coverage for seniors and certain disabled individuals. These programs collectively contribute to improving the quality of life and healthcare access for millions of Americans, helping to ensure financial security and well-being in their later years. Understanding Social Security and Medicare's features, enrollment options, and benefits is essential for individuals planning their retirement and healthcare needs.

CHAPTER 9:

Other Concepts of Health Insurance

9.1 Premium Payment Modes

Premium payment modes refer to the options available to policyholders for paying their health insurance premiums. Insurance companies offer various payment modes to accommodate the preferences and convenience of policyholders. These modes determine how often and through which methods policyholders can make their premium payments. Here are some common modes of premium payment for health insurance:

1. Annual Payment: Policyholders can pay their health insurance premium once a year. This mode offers the convenience of making a single payment for the entire policy year.

2. Semi-Annual Payment: Policyholders make premium payments twice a year in this mode. This option can help individuals budget their premium expenses over two payments.

3. Quarterly Payment: Quarterly premium payment involves making payments every three months. This mode provides more frequent payment options and can help spread the insurance cost over the year.

4. Monthly Payment: Monthly premium payment allows policyholders to pay their insurance premium every month. This is often the most flexible option for budgeting, but it may result in slightly higher administrative costs compared to less frequent payment modes.

5. Payroll Deduction: Many employer-sponsored health insurance plans offer payroll deduction as a convenient way for employees to pay their premiums. The premium amount is deducted directly from the employee's paycheck, making it easy to manage.

6. Electronic Funds Transfer (EFT): Policyholders can set up electronic funds transfer to automatically deduct the premium from their bank account on a specified date each month or quarter.

7. Online Payment: Insurance companies often provide online portals where policyholders can log in and make premium payments using credit cards, debit cards, or electronic checks.

8. Mobile Apps: Some insurance companies offer mobile apps that allow policyholders to make premium payments using their smartphones or other mobile devices.

9. Check or Money Order: Policyholders can pay their premiums by mailing a check or money order to the insurance company.

10. Agent or Office Payment: Policyholders can visit the insurance company's local office or meet with an insurance agent to make premium payments in person.

11. Phone Payment: Some insurance companies offer a phone payment option where policyholders can call a designated phone number to make premium payments using a credit card or bank account.

12. Automatic Credit Card Payment: Policyholders can provide their credit card information to the insurance company for automatic premium payments.

13. Premium Payment Coupons: Policyholders receive payment coupons from the insurance company, which they can use to send their premium payments via mail.

Policyholders must choose a premium payment mode that aligns with their financial situation and preferences. Consistent and timely premium payments are essential to maintain continuous health insurance coverage and ensure access to healthcare services when needed. Insurance companies may offer discounts or incentive payment modes, so policyholders should inquire about available options and associated benefits. Additionally, policyholders should be aware of any grace periods the insurance company provides in case of delayed premium payments to avoid policy lapses.

9.2 Premium Taxations

Health insurance premiums and their taxation can vary based on the country's tax laws, the type of health insurance plan, and the individual's circumstances. Taxation of health insurance premiums may affect the deductibility of premiums for individuals and businesses. Here is an overview of how health insurance premiums are taxed in the United States:

United States: Taxation of Health Insurance Premiums
In the United States, the tax treatment of health insurance premiums depends on whether the premiums are paid with pre-tax or post-tax dollars and whether the insurance is obtained through an employer-sponsored plan or an individual plan.

1. Employer-Sponsored Health Insurance
Pre-Tax Premiums: Many employers offer health insurance benefits as part of their employee benefits package. If the premiums for employer-sponsored health insurance are paid with pre-tax dollars, the contributions are excluded from the employee's gross income. This means that the employee's taxable income is reduced by the premium amount, which can result in lower overall tax liability.

Post-Tax Premiums: If the premiums for employer-sponsored health insurance are paid with post-tax dollars (not through a Section 125 cafeteria plan or other pre-tax arrangement), they are not deductible from the employee's gross income for tax purposes.

2. Individual Health Insurance
For individuals who purchase health insurance on their own (outside of employer-sponsored plans), the tax treatment of premiums depends on whether the individual itemizes deductions on their tax return.

Itemizing Deductions: If an individual itemizes deductions on their federal income tax return, they may be able to deduct a portion of their health insurance premiums as part of their medical expenses. However, medical expenses must exceed a certain threshold (adjusted gross income percentage) before they are deductible.

High-Deductible Health Plans (HDHPs) and Health Savings Accounts (HSAs): Some individuals with high-deductible health plans may be eligible to contribute to Health Savings Accounts (HSAs). Contributions to HSAs are tax-deductible and can be used to pay for qualified medical expenses, including health insurance premiums.

Affordable Care Act (ACA) Tax Credits: Under the Affordable Care Act, individuals and families with low to moderate incomes may be eligible for premium tax credits (subsidies) to help reduce the cost of health insurance premiums when purchasing coverage through the Health Insurance Marketplace.

Self-Employed Individuals: Self-employed People may be able to deduct their health insurance premiums to be a business expense, thus lowering their taxable income.

It is important to note that tax laws and regulations can change, and individuals should consult with a tax professional or financial advisor to understand their health insurance premiums' specific tax implications based on their circumstances. Additionally, health insurance regulations and tax treatments may differ in other countries, so individuals should inquire about the taxation of health insurance premiums in their respective jurisdictions.

9.3 Rights of Owner

Health insurance policyholders, often called policy owners, have certain rights and privileges related to their health insurance coverage. These rights are designed to ensure that policyholders have access to the benefits and services they are entitled to and that their interests are protected throughout their policy. Here are some important rights that health insurance policy owners typically have:

1. Right to Obtain Coverage: Policy owners have the right to apply for and obtain health insurance coverage, subject to the terms and conditions of the insurance company. As long as they meet the eligibility criteria, policyholders can access the benefits specified in their policy.

2. Right to Choose a Plan: Policyholders often have the right to choose from different health insurance plans offered by the insurance company. They can select a plan that best meets their healthcare needs and budget.

3. Right to Review Policy Documents: Health insurance policy owners have the right to receive and review the full policy documents, which outline the coverage details, benefits, limitations, exclusions, and terms of the insurance contract.

4. Right to Privacy and Confidentiality: Policy owners' personal and medical information is protected by privacy laws. Insurance companies must maintain the confidentiality of policyholders' information and use it only for purposes related to the insurance policy.

5. Right to Transparent Information: Policyholders have the right to clear and accurate information about their coverage, including benefits, costs, network providers, claims procedures, and any changes to the policy.

6. Right to Coverage Verification: When policyholders seek medical services, they can verify their coverage and benefits with the insurance company. They can confirm whether a specific treatment or service is covered before receiving care.

7. Right to Timely Claims Processing: Policyholders have the right to timely claims processing. Insurance companies must process and settle valid claims promptly, ensuring that policyholders receive the benefits they are entitled to.

8. Right to Appeal Denials: Policyholders can appeal the decision if a claim is denied or benefits are reduced. Insurance companies must provide a clear process for policyholders to dispute claim denials and seek a review of the decision.

9. Right to Portability and Continuity: In certain cases, policyholders can continue their health insurance coverage when transitioning between plans, employers, or life events. This includes options such as COBRA continuation coverage or transitioning to a new insurance plan without loss of coverage due to pre-existing conditions.

10. Right to cancel or Terminate Coverage: Policyholders have the right to cancel or terminate their health insurance coverage according to the terms of the policy. They can choose to discontinue coverage if it no longer meets their needs.

11. Right to Non-Discrimination: Insurance companies are prohibited from discriminating against policyholders based on age, gender, race, religion, or health status.

12. Right to Advocate for Coverage: Policyholders have the right to advocate for the coverage they believe they are entitled to. They can work with their health care providers and insurance companies to make sure they receive the treatments and services they need.

13. Right to Premium Rate Information: Policyholders can receive information about premium rates, including any changes or increases, before their policy renewal.

14. Right to Obtain Explanation of Benefits (EOB): Policyholders are entitled to receive an Explanation of Benefits (EOB) after a claim is processed. The EOB provides a detailed breakdown of how the claim was handled, including payments made and any amounts owed.

Health insurance policyholders need to be aware of their rights and responsibilities to make informed decisions and ensure they receive their coverage's full benefits and protections. If policyholders encounter any issues or have concerns about their rights, they can contact their insurance company's customer service or seek assistance from regulatory authorities or consumer protection agencies.

9.4 Primary Beneficiaries

In life insurance and certain financial accounts, a primary beneficiary is an individual or entity designated by the policy or account holder to receive the benefits or proceeds in the event of the policyholder's death. The primary beneficiary is the first in line to receive the designated funds or assets, and they have the primary right to the benefits. Designating primary beneficiaries is an important aspect of estate planning and ensuring that one's financial assets are distributed according to their wishes. Here is more information about primary beneficiaries:

1. Types of Policies and Accounts: Primary beneficiaries are commonly designated in various financial instruments, including:

- **Life Insurance Policies:** In life insurance policies, the primary beneficiary is the person or entity receiving the death benefit when the insured person dies.

- **Retirement Accounts:** For retirement accounts such as IRAs (Individual Retirement Accounts) and 401(k) s, the primary beneficiary is the individual or entity entitled to inherit the account's assets upon the account holder's death.

- **Payable-On-Death (POD) Accounts:** In bank accounts or investment accounts with a POD designation, the primary beneficiary is the person who will receive the account balance upon the account holder's death.

- **Transfer-On-Death (TOD) Accounts:** Similar to POD accounts, TOD accounts designate a primary beneficiary to inherit the assets in the account after the account holder's death.

2. Designation and Change: The policy or account holder designates the primary beneficiary when setting up the policy or account. This designation can usually be changed during the policy or account holder's lifetime. Beneficiary designations can be updated to reflect changes in personal circumstances, such as marriage, divorce, the birth of children, or changes in relationships.

3. Contingent Beneficiary: Besides primary beneficiaries, policy and account holders can also designate contingent beneficiaries. A contingent beneficiary will benefit if the primary beneficiary predeceases the policy or account holder. Contingent beneficiaries are a backup if the primary beneficiary does not receive the benefits.

4. Distribution upon Death: Upon the policy or account holder's death, the primary beneficiary (or contingent beneficiary, if applicable) typically must provide appropriate documentation to the insurance company or financial institution to claim the benefits. Once the required documentation is submitted and verified, the benefits or assets are distributed to the beneficiary.

5. Estate Planning Considerations: Dividing primary beneficiaries is crucial. It allows individuals to specify who will inherit their financial assets and ensures they are distributed according to their wishes. It may also have implications for estate taxes and probate.

6. Revocable and Irrevocable Designations: In some cases, beneficiary designations may be revocable or irrevocable. A revocable designation allows the policy or account holder to change beneficiaries anytime. On the other hand, an irrevocable designation may require the beneficiary's consent before changes can be made.

Policy and account holders must periodically review and update their beneficiary designations, especially when major life events occur. Professional advice can help people make informed decisions about beneficiary designations and ensure their wishes are properly documented and executed.

9.5 Benefits for Dependent Children

Dependent children benefits are provisions within health insurance policies that provide coverage for the medical expenses and healthcare needs of children who are dependents of the policyholder. Typically, dependent children include the policyholder's biological or adopted children, stepchildren, or foster children. These benefits ensure children access necessary healthcare services, treatments, and preventive care.

Key Points

- Dependent children benefits may cover doctor visits, hospitalizations, prescription medications, vaccinations, and preventive care.

- Coverage may extend to routine check-ups, immunizations, dental and vision care, and specialist consultations.

- Eligibility criteria and age limits for dependent children coverage vary between insurance plans.

- Dependent children benefits are essential for families when selecting a health insurance plan.

9.6 Recurrent and Residual Disability

Recurrent and residual disability clauses are important components of disability insurance policies that address specific scenarios related to recurring disabilities or reduced earning capacity.

Key Points

- **Recurrent Disability:** This clause specifies how benefits are handled if the insured experiences a recurrence of the same disability within a certain timeframe after the initial disability has ended. Some policies may provide continued coverage, while others might consider the recurrence as part of the original disability period.

- **Residual Disability:** Residual disability benefits come into play when the insured can work but experiences a reduced income due to a disability. These benefits provide partial coverage for the loss of income, bridging the gap between pre-disability and post-disability earnings.

9.7 Total and Partial Disability

Total and partial disability provisions are found in disability insurance policies and describe the conditions under which an insured individual is considered very disabled or partially disabled. These provisions determine the insured's benefits based on their ability to work and earn an income.

Key Points

- **Total Disability:** Total disability refers to a condition where the insured person cannot perform substantial or gainful work due to injury or illness. Benefits for total disability are usually more comprehensive and provide a higher level of financial support.

- **Partial Disability:** Partial disability refers to a condition where the insured can work but cannot perform their regular occupation or earn their full pre-disability income. Benefits for partial disability are typically proportionate to the reduction in earning capacity.

9.8 Managed Care

Managed care is a healthcare delivery system designed to control costs and improve the quality of care by coordinating medical services, promoting preventive care, and managing healthcare utilization.

Key Points

- Managed care plans include Preferred Provider Organizations (PPOs), Point of Service (POS) plans and Health Maintenance Organizations (HMOs).

- HMOs demand members select a PCP (primary care doctor) and obtain referrals to specialists from the PCP.

- PPOs offer more flexibility in the choice of healthcare specialists and providers, but higher out-of-pocket costs may apply for out-of-network care.

- POS plans combine features of HMOs and PPOs, allowing policyholders to choose between in-network and out-of-network assistance.

9.9 Subrogation

Subrogation is a legal principle allowing an insurance company to recover payments made to the insured or a third party on behalf of the insured. It typically applies when the insured person receives compensation from a liable third party, such as in personal injury or medical malpractice cases.

Key Points

- When an insurance company pays a claim for the insured due to a covered event, it may have the right to recover the amount paid from any responsible third party.

- Subrogation prevents the insured from receiving a double recovery (benefits from the insurance company and a third party).

- Subrogation clauses vary by insurance type and jurisdiction. They are often included in health insurance policies, auto insurance, and other types of coverage.

Understanding these health insurance concepts is important for policyholders to make informed decisions about their coverage, benefits, and potential financial implications in various situations. It is recommended to review policy documents and consult with insurance professionals or experts to fully grasp the details of these provisions.

CHAPTER 10:

Studying Tips and Tricks for the Life and Health Insurance Examination

Preparing for a life and health insurance exam can be a challenging endeavor, requiring a combination of effective study strategies, time management, and stress reduction techniques. This chapter will delve into valuable insights and practical tips to help you pass the exam on your first attempt, reduce test anxiety, and excel during the written examination.

10.1 Tips for Passing the Exam on the First Go

The goal of passing the life and health insurance exam on your initial attempt demands focused effort, dedication, and a well-structured study approach. Here are some indispensable tips to increase your chances of success:

- **Develop a Study Plan:** Constructing a comprehensive study plan is paramount. Divide the course material into manageable chunks, and give each area of material its time slot. A structured study plan will help you cover all necessary areas effectively.

- **Utilize Reliable Resources:** Choose study materials, textbooks, online courses, and practice exams from reputable sources that align with the exam's content. Ensuring the quality and accuracy of your study materials is crucial.

- **Conceptual Understanding:** Rather than memorization, strive to deeply understand key concepts. This approach empowers you to apply your knowledge to real-world scenarios, enhancing your problem-solving skills.

- **Practice Consistently:** Regular practice with sample questions and mock exams is instrumental in building familiarity with the exam format, improving time management, and boosting confidence.

- **Frequent Review:** Set aside dedicated time for reviewing previously covered material. Regular revision solidifies your grasp of concepts and reinforces your memory.

- **Teach and Explain:** Sharing your knowledge with others, whether a study partner or yourself, helps reinforce your understanding and identify areas requiring further clarification.

- **Prioritize Well-being:** Your physical and mental health is vital to effective studying. Prioritize sleep, engage in regular physical activity, and maintain a balanced diet to optimize your cognitive functioning.

- **Stress Management:** Break your study sessions into manageable chunks, take short breaks, and use relaxation techniques to prevent burnout. Maintain a positive mindset and believe in your ability to succeed.

10.2 How Can You Get Rid of Test Anxiety?

Test anxiety can hinder your performance on the exam, but adopting effective strategies can help manage and mitigate this anxiety:

- **Preparedness is Key:** Thoroughly preparing by studying the material boosts your confidence, reducing anxiety associated with the fear of the unknown.

- **Deep Breathing:** Practice breathing exercises before and during the exam to calm your nerves and maintain focus.

- **Positive Visualization:** Visualize yourself successfully navigating the exam. Positive imagery can alleviate anxiety and enhance your self-assurance.

- **Positive Self-talk:** Replace negative thoughts with positive affirmations. Believe in your preparation and trust your capabilities.

- **Time Management:** Arrive early at the exam location to prevent additional stress. Adequate time ensures you can settle in and familiarize yourself with the environment.

- **Stay Present:** Concentrate on the question in front of you. Avoid being caught up in worrying about future questions.

10.3 The Most Effective Tips for Passing the Written Exam

As you approach the written examination, consider these invaluable tips to optimize your performance:

- **Thoroughly Read Instructions:** Begin by carefully reading and understanding the instructions provided. This ensures you are aware of the structure and time constraints of the exam.

- **Preview the Exam:** Quickly skim through all the questions to gain an overview of the content. This initial preview can help you allocate your time more efficiently.

- **Start with Confidence:** Begin with questions you find easier or more familiar. This builds momentum and boosts your self-assurance.

- **Effective Time Allocation:** Allocate an appropriate amount of time to each question. Avoid spending excessive time on a single question that may hinder your progress.

- **Eliminate Wrong Choices:** If uncertain about an answer, use the process of elimination to narrow down your options. This increases your likelihood of selecting the correct answer.

- **Review Your Work:** If time permits, revisit your answers to ensure accuracy and completeness. Correct any errors or incomplete responses.

- **Maintain Calm:** Stay composed and avoid succumbing to panic when encountering challenging questions. Overthinking can lead to confusion.

- **Trust Yourself:** Have confidence in your preparation and trust your instincts. You have dedicated time and effort to excel on the exam.

In conclusion, effectively preparing for a life and health insurance exam requires a multifaceted approach encompassing diligent study, stress management, and strategic test-taking techniques. Adhering to these tips and tricks can enhance your study routine, mitigate test anxiety, and optimize your performance during the written examination. Remember that preparation and a positive mindset are paramount to achieving success. Good luck with your exam journey!

CHAPTER 11:

Practice Tests for the Life and Health Examination

Choose the best possible answer from the responses that are available

11.1 Quiz Number 1

1) A rider to the disability income policy for social insurance benefits (SIS)...

1. Only pays benefits if it comes out that the insured is eligible for social insurance benefits.
2. Pays a benefit if the insured suffers a work-related injury and qualifies for workers' compensation.
3. Provides a benefit only if the insured is completely disabled and receives no social insurance benefits.
4. Provides a matching incentive payment for social security disability income benefits, if paid.

2) To contain costs, a health maintenance organization (HMO) plan promotes...

1. After-hours care
2. General Assistance
3. Preventative assistance
4. Paid assistance

3) A $50,000 whole-life policy with a $10,000 cash value has lasted eleven years. The policyholder is unable to continue paying the premium. What best characterizes the reduced paid-up no forfeiture option?

1. The policyholder begins receiving $200 monthly payments for life from the insurer
2. The policyholder surrenders the policy and receives $10,000 from the insurer
3. The cash value purchases a paid-up, 10-year, $50,000 term policy
4. The cash value is used to purchase a paid-up policy for $20,000

4) Typically, term insurance is characterized by:

1. Low premiums and a substantial cash value
2. Exorbitant premiums with no cash value
3. Exorbitant premiums and cash value
4. Low premiums without cash value

5) All of the following are typical provisions for life insurance policies, except for:

1. Extended duration
2. Certainty of insurability
3. Accidental fatality
4. Exemption from premium

6) A proportionate sharing provision specifies that healthcare insureds & their insurance companies will share the losses covered in an agreed-upon proportion. Is called:

1. The stop-loss clause
2. All-inclusive coverage
3. Percentage of coverage
4. Coinsurance is a proportional sharing provision

7) When an authorized agent applies for renewal and the necessary fee before the end date,...

1. The agent may conduct business if the payment receipt is returned before the license expiration date
2. The agent may operate for up to 60 days after the expiration date specified
3. The agent can operate if they visit the insurance department in person to receive a provisional license extension
4. If requested and approved, the agent may continue to operate after a 30-day extension without a receipt

8) A hospitalization indemnity insurance policy pays:

1. Reimbursement to the insured for all hospitalization-related expenses
2. The daily benefit coverage amount specified in the policy is for every day the insured is hospitalized
3. One hundred percent of covered medical expenses, less the deductible and coinsurance proportion
4. The actual hospital expenses incurred

9) Which of the following represents a risk?

1. An abundance of identical exposure units
2. A threat
3. A circumstance that may increase the probability of a loss occurring
4. Speculative danger

10) Which of the following costs is never covered by long-term care insurance?

1. In-home medical services
2. Senior daycare
3. The hospital's intensive care unit
4. Alzheimer's illness

11) The California insurance code stipulates that an insured's policy must include all of the following, except:

1. The hazards insured against
2. The insurer's financial rating
3. The property or life being insured
4. The duration of the policy

12) What is a health insurance deductible?

1. The insured's payment for non-covered healthcare services
2. The cost of covered services minus the office co-payment
3. The portion of the premium paid by the insured for coverage
4. The amount of covered expenses the insured pays before the insurer's payment.

13) Which of the following are typically included in medical expense policies?

1. Cosmetic procedures of choice
2. Existing medical conditions
3. Costs covered by employees' compensation insurance
4. Accidental injuries

14) To receive the principal sum death benefit from a disability policy, the insured must pass away...

1. Within a predetermined number of days after the injury
2. At any point during the rehabilitation period
3. At any time during a total dismemberment period
4. During the duration of the policy, for any reason

15) A metric for assessing a person's need for LTC benefits is known as:

1. Case administration
2. Daily living activities
3. The gatekeeper mechanism
4. Shared-risk

11.1.1 Answer key of Quiz Number 1

1) Answer: 3. Supplemental Security Income, sometimes known as SSI, is a form of extra income support that is only provided if the insured person is completely incapacitated and receives no other form of social insurance benefits.

2) Answer: 3. Preventative care. A Health Maintenance Organization (HMO) plan reduces costs by promoting preventative care, which focuses on preventing illnesses and addressing health issues before they become severe and require expensive treatments.

3) Answer: 4. With the reduced paid-up no forfeiture option, the cash value can be put towards the purchase of a paid-up insurance for the amount of $20,000; however, this choice results in a lower death benefit but eliminates the requirement that additional premium payments be made.

4) Answer: 4. Low premiums without cash value. Term insurance is characterized by low premiums and no cash value accumulation. It provides coverage for a specific term and is designed to provide temporary protection.

5) Answer: 1. The term "extended duration" does not refer to a regular feature of life insurance plans or contracts.

6) Answer: 4. Coinsurance is a proportional sharing provision. Coinsurance is a provision where the insured and the insurer share covered losses in an agreed proportion. It helps to prevent the overutilization of insurance benefits.

7) Answer: 2. The agent may operate for up to 60 days after the expiration date specified. Suppose an authorized representative presents an application for renewal and fee before expiration. In that case, they may continue operating for sixty days after the receipt's expiration date.

8) Answer: 2. The daily benefit coverage amount specified in the policy is for every day the insured is hospitalized. A hospitalization indemnity insurance policy pays a daily benefit amount for each day the insured is hospitalized, providing financial support during hospital stays.

9) Answer: 3. A circumstance that may increase the probability of a loss. A risk refers to a circumstance that may increase the probability of a loss occurring, potentially leading to negative consequences.

10) Answer: 3. Hospital's intensive care unit. Long-term care insurance typically does not cover the hospital's intensive care unit expenses, as it focuses on covering long-term care services such as assistance with daily living activities.

11) Answer: 2. The insurer's financial rating. The California insurance code requires an insured's policy to include the hazards insured against, the property or life insured, and the duration of the policy, but not the insurer's financial rating.

12) Answer: 4. The amount of covered expenses the insured pays before the insurer's payment. A health insurance deductible is the amount the insured must pay for covered medical expenses before the insurer's payments begin.

13) Answer: 4. Accidental injuries. Medical expense policies typically cover costs associated with accidental injuries, not existing medical conditions or cosmetic procedures.

14) Answer: 1. Within a predetermined number of days after the injury. Explanation: To receive the principal sum death benefit from a disability policy, the insured must pass away within a predetermined number of days after the injury.

15) Answer: 2. Daily living activities. Activities of daily living (ADLs) are a metric for assessing a person's need for long-term care (LTC) benefits, reflecting their ability to perform basic tasks independently.

11.2 Quiz Number 2

1) Which definition of disability is the most challenging for a worker to meet?

1. The Social Security Administration's personal occupation definition
2. The standard definition of partial disability utilized by disability benefit policies
3. The Social Security Administration's comprehensive disability definition

2) What authority does the Insurance Commissioner have if an agent needs more authority from an insurer named on a coverage binder?

1. Fine the insurance company for noncompliance
2. Suspend or revoke the agent's license
3. Provide the agent with a certificate of convenience
4. Immediately request that a certificate of authority be issued

3) If an insurer cannot satisfy financial obligations when they are due, the insurer is considered:

1. Insolvent
2. Unapproved
3. Limitation
4. Non-admissible

4) The following statements concerning survivorship life insurance are all true, except

1. Typical policy values are greater than $1,000,000
2. When the first covered person dies, the policy will pay out the full-face value
3. It offers premiums that are significantly less than those of distinct policies
4. It is ideally suited to satisfy the requirements of estate taxes

5) The insured suffers from a total and permanent disability. The policy of the insured remains in effect without premium payment because it contains a:

1. Grace period clause
2. Provision guaranteeing insurability
3. Premium waiver provision
4. reinstatement clause

6) The payer clause on a juvenile life insurance policy stipulates that if the payer dies or becomes disabled before the insured juvenile reaches the specified age on the policy...

1. The insurer will make payments until the insured child reaches the specified age
2. The insurer will provide a loan to maintain the policy active
3. The insured's estate will make the premium payments
4. The insurer will handle all premium payments

7) Each of the following statements about contingent beneficiaries is true, except one.

1. They receive remaining payments to be made under a settlement agreement upon the death of the primary beneficiary
2. They share death proceeds equally with the primary beneficiary
3. They receive the death proceeds if the primary beneficiary died at the time of the insured's death
4. More than one contingent beneficiary may be named

8) A form or relief offered to family members who provide continuous care for a loved one is called

1. Palliative care
2. Hospital treatment
3. Temporary maintenance
4. Intermediate treatment

9) An illustration of a third-party administrator is:

1. A superintendent of an agent who shares in his commission
2. An employee who manages claims for self-insurance
3. An employee responsible for assessing the relative quality of competing group health and welfare benefits offered by insurers to his employer
4. A third-party organization that processes claims for an employer's self-funded plans

10) A person with a low income and significant insurance requirements should purchase:

1. Whole life insurance
2. Universal life insurance
3. Endowment life insurance
4. Term coverage

11) Which clause does pay a portion of the death benefit before the insured's death from a severe illness?

1. Premium Waiver
2. Accelerated Death Benefit
3. Living Costs
4. Disability Income

12) The probationary period in a group health insurance policy is designed for:

1. Those who joined the group after the policy's effective date
2. Those who experienced a qualifying incident but did not enroll during their eligibility window
3. Those who have a pre-existing condition upon joining the group

13) RW and Associates is the insurance agency for BLG Insurance Corporation. RW and Associates may leave BLG Insurance Corporation's name in its advertisements so long as the relationship between the two companies is made evident in one of the following ways:

1. RW & Associates, BLG Insurance Corporation
2. RW and Associates provide underwriting services for BLG Insurance Corporation
3. RW & Associates utilizing the services of BLG Insurance Corporation
4. RW and Associates are utilizing BLG Insurance Corporation's services

14) The enactment of worker's compensation legislation meant:

1. Employees had no legal recourse to receive compensation for work-related injuries
2. Employees must sue their employers to receive compensation for work-related injuries
3. Employers would be liable for the cost of work-related injuries regardless of the fault
4. Employers were no longer liable for employees' work-related injuries

15) Which insurance policy type ensures policy renewal every year, regardless of the insured's health, for a slightly higher premium?

1. Term convertible
2. Term Level
3. Term Decreasing
4. Term Renewal

11.2.1 Answer key of Quiz Number 2

1) Answer: 3. To be eligible for disability benefits from the Social Security Administration, an individual must meet the agency's stringent standards for showing total disability, which includes the incapacity to engage in any substantial gainful activity.

2) Answer: 2. Suspend or revoke the agent's license. If an agent needs more authority from an insurer named on a coverage binder and fails to comply, the Insurance Commissioner has the authority to suspend or revoke the agent's license.

3) Answer: 1. Insolvent. If an insurer cannot satisfy financial obligations when due, it is considered insolvent, meaning it cannot pay its debts and financial obligations.

4) Answer: 2. Survivorship life insurance guarantees that the remaining insured or beneficiaries will receive the full death benefit if the policyholder dies before the policy matures.

5) Answer: 4. If the insured becomes fully and permanently incapacitated and is unable to pay premiums, the policy may be reinstated under the terms of the policy's reinstatement clause.

6) Answer: 1. The insurer will make payments until the insured child reaches the specified age. The payer clause ensures that if the payer dies or becomes disabled, the insurer will make payments until the insured child reaches the specified age.

7) Answer: 2. They share death proceeds equally with the primary beneficiary. Contingent beneficiaries receive death proceeds if the primary beneficiary is deceased but do not necessarily share death proceeds equally with the primary beneficiary.

8) Answer: 3. Temporary maintenance. Respite care provides temporary relief to family members by providing continuous care for a loved one, allowing them to take a break from caregiving responsibilities.

9) Answer: 4. A third-party organization that processes claims for an employer's self-funded plans. A third-party administrator (TPA) processes claims for self-funded plans on behalf of employers, assisting in the administration of employee benefits.

10) Answer: 4. Term coverage. A person with low income and significant insurance requirements may choose term coverage due to its lower initial premiums than permanent life insurance.

11) Answer: 2. Accelerated Death Benefit. The accelerated death benefit clause pays a portion of the death benefit before the insured's death in the case of a severe illness or condition.

12) Answer: 1. Those who joined the group after the policy's effective date. The probationary period in a group health insurance policy is designed for individuals who join the group after the policy's effective date.

13) Answer: 2. The statement "RLG Insurance Corporation is a client of RW and Associates, which provides underwriting services," clarifies the basis of the partnership between RW and Associates & BLG Insurance Corporation.

14) Answer: 3. Employers would be liable for the cost of work-related injuries regardless of fault. The enactment of worker's compensation legislation established that employers would be liable for the cost of work-related injuries regardless of fault, ensuring compensation for injured employees.

15) Answer: 4. Term Renewal. Term Renewal guarantees the right to renew the policy annually, regardless of health, for a higher premium.

11.3 Quiz Number 3

1) Which action is available to the injured party for intentional concealment?

1. None since the concealment was accidental.
2. A sanction of $250 must be paid to the injured party
3. Possibility of imprisonment for the individual who concealed information
4. Cancellation of the agreement

2) Several decades ago, the insured purchased a $150,000 non-participating whole-life policy. Today, he turns 100 years old. He has never borrowed against the policy's cash value and has carefully made all payments when due. The cash value of the policy is:

1. $150,000
2. $100,000
3. $0
4. $50,000

3) What would be the most probable course of action taken by the Insurance Commissioner if an applicant for an insurance license had a previous application for a professional license denied for cause within five years of the date of filing?

1. Probably deny the application after a hearing
2. The application will be approved if it is unrelated to insurance
3. Approve only following evaluation by a panel of insurance experts
4. Refuse the request without a hearing

4) What purpose does "key person" insurance serve?

1. To offer essential employees health insurance benefits
2. To permit a key employee to acquire the company.
3. To offer retirement benefits to essential personnel
4. To compensate for diminished business revenues caused by the demise of a key employee

5) All of the following statements regarding the selection of settlement options for a life insurance policy are true, except for:

1. The policyholder makes the selection when the application is submitted
2. If no resolution is chosen, the money will go to the state where the policyholder resides
3. The policyholder can alter the settlement option after it has been selected
4. If no payment option was in place at the time following the insured's death, the beneficiary can make the decision

6) Which of the following best describes an insurer with sufficient financial resources to cover all its liabilities and all reinsurance obligations?

1. Certainty guaranteed
2. Insolvable
3. Ingredient
4. Not taking part

7) What options does an insurer have if a breach of a material warranty by the insured is discovered?

1. An investigation by the insurance commissioner to ascertain the gravity of the misrepresentation and the proper course of action
2. None of the policy has been in effect for over a year
3. Cancellation of the policy
4. A court proceeding to ascertain the appropriate course of action for an insurer

8) What differences exist between the privileges of an irrevocable beneficiary and those of a revocable beneficiary?

1. A policyholder may alter an irrevocable beneficiary without the beneficiary's consent
2. An irrevocable beneficiary has a right that neither the policyholder nor his creditors can impair without the beneficiary's permission
3. A beneficiary with revocable rights can acquire the policy anytime by paying the premiums
4. An irrevocable beneficiary may designate a contingent beneficiary for the insurance policy

9) A managed care indemnity plan's defining characteristic is that participants:

1. Identify a provider and submit claims to the insurer
2. Select a workplace provider and claims processor
3. Select a doctor and third-party claims administrator in advance
4. Select a clinic in advance and submit claims to the insurance provider

10) Renewable term insurance is most accurately characterized as:

1. A flat mortality benefit with a rising premium
2. A constant mortality benefit with a declining premium
3. A diminishing mortality benefit with a fixed premium
4. A rising mortality benefit with a constant premium

11) Which of the following is a financial need rather than an income need?

1. Fund for estate clearance
2. Adjustment interval
3. Dependency interval
4. Lifetime payment for a spouse

12) Level premium strategy...

1. Involves paying excessively during the initial years of the contract
2. Offers permanent protection
3. Demands the formation of a legal reserve
4. Is a byproduct of the policy's savings
5. All of the preceding

13) Everything is true regarding the annually renewable term technique except for:

1. The premium is each individual's share of the total cost of death
2. Term insurance premiums increase with age
3. Premiums tend to rise at an accelerating rate
4. It is a sensible way to afford everlasting protection
5. None of the preceding

14) Which type of annuity should a woman who has taught music and has no close relatives or friends purchase? (Assume that the woman wishes to maximize her annuity income)

1. Join the lone survivor.
2. Whole Existence
3. Cash reimbursement
4. Certain for fifteen years and life
5. Twenty certain years and existence

15) In how many of the following ways is a 20-payment life insurance policy dissimilar to a 20-year endowment? I. The amount payable should the insured die within 20 years. II. The number of premiums paid. III. The amount payable to the insured if he is still alive at the end of 20 years.

1. I alone
2. the only Three
3. I and Two
4. I and Three
5. I, II, then III

11.3.1 Answer key of Quiz Number 3

1) Answer: 4. If one party intentionally withholds material information from the other, the contract may be null and unenforceable due to the lack of good faith and full disclosure, leaving the injured party with only the option of terminating the agreement.

2) Answer: 1. $150,000. The policy's cash value is typically equal to the face amount of the policy if the insured reaches a certain age (e.g., 100 years old) without utilizing the cash value or borrowing against it.

3) Answer: 4. If an applicant has had a professional license application denied for cause within the past five years, the Insurance Commissioner is likely to deny their request for an insurance license outright, without even holding a hearing.

4) Answer: 4. To compensate for diminished business revenues caused by the demise of a key employee. "Key person" insurance provides coverage to compensate for potential financial losses that a business may incur due to the death of a key employee.

5) Answer: 2. When it comes to unclaimed life insurance proceeds, the assertion that "if no resolution is chosen, the money will go to the state where the policyholder resides" is usually not accurate. Instead, the insurer will usually hold onto the money until a valid beneficiary claim is made.

6) Answer: 2. An insurer is termed "solvent" (financially stable) and not "insolvent" (unable to pay claims and reinsurance) if it has adequate assets to do so.

7) Answer: 3. Cancellation of the policy. If a breach of a material warranty by the insured is discovered, one of the options available to the insurer is canceling the policy.

8) Answer: 2. An irrevocable beneficiary has a right that neither the policyholder nor his creditors can impair without the beneficiary's permission. An irrevocable beneficiary has certain rights protected from changes by the policyholder or creditors without the beneficiary's consent.

9) Answer: 1. Identify a provider and submit claims to the insurer. A managed care indemnity plan requires participants to identify a healthcare provider and submit claims to the insurer for reimbursement.

10) Answer: 1. The best way to describe renewable term insurance is as having a flat mortality benefit with a growing premium, meaning that the death benefit stays the same but the premium does each time the policy is renewed.

11) Answer: 1. Fund for estate clearance. A fund for estate clearance is a financial need, as it helps cover expenses related to the settlement of an individual's estate after their passing.

12) Answer: 5. All of the preceding. The level premium strategy involves paying higher premiums initially, offers permanent protection, requires the formation of a legal reserve, and generates cash value over time.

13) Answer: 4. It is a sensible way to afford everlasting protection. There are more sensible ways to afford everlasting protection than the yearly renewable term method since premiums tend to accelerate over time.

14) Answer: 2. Since she likely does not have any close family or acquaintances to whom she could leave her remaining assets, the woman in this situation would be well advised to consider acquiring a "Whole Existence" annuity.

15) Answer: 2. The sole difference between a 20-payment life insurance policy and a 20-year endowment is the amount of premiums paid (III).

11.4 Quiz Number 4

1) A life insurance contract includes the following parties, except for:

1. Underwriter
2. Insurer
3. Beneficiary
4. Owner
5. Insured
6. 1 and 3

2) For a policy to be issued, which of the following must satisfy an insurable interest requirement?

1. The insured
2. the beneficiary
3. the insured's dependents
4. all of the above
5. Just both 1 and 2

3) Jack recently bought a house with a 15-year mortgage, along with his wife Lyn. Jack's "temporary" requirement for life insurance was to ensure that Lyn would be able to cover the mortgage balance in the case of his death. What kind of insurance ought Jack to buy?

1. Whole Life Protection
2. Insurance on Term Life
3. Insurance on Variable Life
4. An Asymmetric Agreement

4) Based on its investment component, which kind of life insurance is deemed riskier?

1. Term Life Insurance at Level
2. Whole Life Protection Reduced
3. Term Life Insurance
4. Insurance on Variable Life

5) Many characteristics are considered by life insurance underwriters before accepting an application. These elements may consist of:

1. A person's medical history
2. Their occupation
3. Their hobbies
4. All of the above
5. Just 1 and 2

6) For an underwriter to issue an insurance policy, which of the following must have an insurable interest?

1. Owner
2. Insurance
3. Beneficiary
4. Insured

7) Which of the following describes a group of connections in which an individual is permitted to act on behalf of another to establish a legal connection with a third party?

1. The laws of principals
2. Agencies
3. Third parties
4. None of the above

8) The quantity of life insurance required may alter as a result of any of the following life-altering occurrences, except for:

1. A child's birth
2. Divorce
3. Marriage
4. A change in employment title

9) Buy/sell agreements should always include term life insurance.

1. True
2. False

10) The following uses are permitted for the proceeds from a corporate-owned life insurance policy:

1. To locate, hire, and onboard a new executive or staff member
2. To pay off additional company debt
3. Redeeming the stock of the deceased employee
4. All of above

11) What is the element that all life insurance policies have in common the most?

1. Living benefits
2. Premium waivers
3. Death benefits
4. Living rider costs are all included

12) There are always two parts to permanent life insurance coverage. How do they look?

1. Benefit of death
2. Value in cash
3. Living Allowances
4. Benefit of Conversion
5. 1 and 2

13) What amount will a life insurance policy beneficiary get upon the insured's passing?

1. Cash value
2. Value at surrender
3. Amount invested
4. Death benefit

14) On August 31, John, who had a life insurance policy with a death payout, passed away following a protracted battle with cancer. Before his passing, he spent a month in the hospital. Following John's funeral on September 5th, her spouse made contact with the insurance company to initiate her claim for the death benefit. This was done after she had had some time to gather her thoughts and address her emotional grief. On October 30th, the insurance agent settled the death benefit by filing the necessary paperwork with his supervisor to complete the claim. In this case, were there any legal violations?

1. No, the documentation was submitted by the agent within 30 days of the claim
2. The claim was, in fact, not resolved within the allotted thirty days
3. No, there are questions regarding John's death
4. Indeed, the claim was not resolved within the allotted 15 days

15) Which of the following is a rider that permits a person who is near death to receive at least some of the earnings from a death benefit before passing away?

1. Living benefit
2. Waiver
3. Complement
4. Addendum

11.4.1 Answer key of Quiz Number 4

1) Answer: 6. The beneficiary and underwriter are not life insurance contract parties. Insurers can be parties, but not always. A wife can ensure her husband, but the husband isn't a participant in the arrangement.

2) Answer: 2. Besides the applicant's details, underwriters will examine the policy's beneficiary to see if there is an insurable interest. If not, life insurance may be denied.

3) Answer: 2. The 15-year term life insurance plan would be best for Jack because the premiums would be much lower than a permanent policy and he would no longer need coverage after the mortgage is paid off.

4) Answer: 4. Variable life insurance policies are securities since they invest in investments like mutual funds. As the equities market fluctuates, variable life insurance is more dangerous than other policies because the investment component may lose value.

5) Answer: 4. Underwriters consider various elements when assessing life insurance applicants' risk. Some characteristics include interests, occupation, lifestyle, gender, age, income, and more.

6) Answer: 3. Policy acceptance is affected by the recipient. The beneficiary must be at risk of loss if the insured dies.

7) Answer: 2. Agents' relationships with principals and third parties on the principal's behalf are governed by agency law.

8) Answer: 4. A new position with a major salary change or dangerous activities may modify life insurance needs, but changing work titles will not.

9) Answer: 2. Permanent life insurance with buy/sell agreements ensures that the insured does not need to re-qualify after a specified time.

10) Answer: 4 The money that is received from a policy of corporately owned life insurance can be put to a variety of uses.

11) Answer: 3. Although life insurance policies can be customized in a great number of ways and include a variety of riders, each one includes a death benefit.

12) Answer: 5. Both a death benefit and a cash value component are included in permanent life insurance policies. The death benefit is paid out to the insured after their passing.

13) Answer: 4. The sum that is paid out as the death benefit to the beneficiary of the policy after the insured passes away is known as the death benefit. If the policyholder of a permanent life insurance policy chooses to terminate the policy before the insured person's passing, the policyholder is entitled to receive the sum equal to the cash surrender value.

14) Answer: 2. Although death benefit claims usually take two weeks to settle, insurance firms must do so within 30 days. Claims that require further investigation may take longer. John's death is unremarkable here.

15) Answer: 1. A life insurance living benefit rider allows an insured with a qualifying terminal illness to use death benefit money to pay medical bills or other expenses. The insured's withdrawals lower the policy's death benefit.

11.5 Quiz Number 5

1) From a legal standpoint, insurance is a contract:

1. In exchange for the policyholder's premium payment, the insurer undertakes to pay the policyholder a specified amount in the event of a covered event

2. This enables the policyholder to pay a small, fixed amount known as the premium in exchange for protection against small, fixed losses

3. Indemnifying the policyholder against minor variable losses for which the policyholder pays a variable premium

4. This enables the insured to pay a fixed premium in exchange for protection against minor, certain losses

5. Wherein the insured takes on the risk of a significant and potentially devastating loss in return for a relatively little and certain payment, the premium

2) Whoever receives the death benefit from an insurance policy is called:

1. Retired person

2. Benefit recipient

3. Covered by insurance

4. A representative for contingency claims

5. None of the preceding

3) An insurance policy that guarantees the policyholder a periodic payout if they remain alive is called

1. Life Insurance Coverage

2. Healthcare Coverage

3. Lifetime Annuity

4. Property Insurance

5. Life Insurance Assurance

4) What are the different types of life and health insurance?

1. Group coverage

2. Normal insurance

3. Credit coverage

4. All of the preceding

5. Only 1 and 3 exist

5) Which of the following are not required for optimal insurance market competition:

1. Numerous buyers and vendors, such that neither a single buyer nor a single seller, nor any other group, can affect the market
2. Insurance providers are allowed to enter and exit the market
3. Buyers and vendors have complete product knowledge
4. Government regulators can specify the pricing for prospective insureds' guaranteed coverage
5. Sellers manufacture identical goods

6) There are economies of magnitude in the insurance industry when:

1. The average cost of production for an insurer decreases as production rises
2. The average cost of production for an insurer rises as production rises
3. The average cost of production for an insurer declines as production declines
4. The marginal cost of production for an insurer is less than the average cost of sales
5. The marginal cost of production for an insurer rises as sales declines

7) Price discrimination is exhibited when:

1. Customers favor the products of one company over those of its adversaries
2. A single company can produce multiple goods or services at lower costs than multiple companies can
3. A company offers essentially identical products at varying prices to distinct groups
4. The average cost of production for an insurer declines as production rises
5. None of a company's products is preferred over its competitors

8) All of the following, except for one, are part of a typical long-term care insurance package.

1. Round of Eliminations
2. Money Received
3. Own profession
4. Duration of Benefits

9) The insurance "lemons" problem occurs when:

1. The customer must know more about the insurance company and its products than the insurer (seller)
2. The customer knows more about the insurance company and its products than the insurer (seller)
3. Poorer-than-average risks pursue insurance at premiums higher than average
4. Individuals modify their conduct due to the availability of insurance
5. Insurers endeavor to sell customers' policies with greater coverage at rates below the norm

10) In insurance, the principal-agent problem occurs when:

1. The customer must know more about the insurance company and its products than the insurer (seller)
2. Poorer-than-average hazards will seek insurance at higher-than-average premiums
3. Individuals attempt to obtain insurance through deception
4. Insurers want to eliminate agents too expensive to keep on the books because they sell too many policies
5. The agent understands their actions better than the principal does; in this case, the insurer does

11) A significant medical insurance coverage must meet various conditions, including:

1. Policy deductible
2. Out-of-pocket maximum
3. Period of elimination
4. All the aforementioned
5. 1 and 2 only

12) Insurance rules are mostly determined by:

1. International level
2. National level
3. State level
4. Local level

13) Applicants for insurance must be given advance notice that includes all of the following, except:

1. The individuals collecting the information
2. The type of information to be collected
3. The sources of information
4. The individuals who have access to personal information

14) Which of the following does not include provisions safeguarding individual privacy?

1. The Gramm-Leach-Bliley Act;
2. The Privacy Act of 1974;
3. The McCarran-Ferguson Act;
4. The Fair Credit Reporting Act.

15) Consumer reporting agencies are prohibited from including the following information in their reports:

1. Bankruptcies older than 14 years;
2. Lawsuits and judgments older than 10 years if the statute of limitations has not expired;
3. Arrests, indictments, or convictions of crime reports; and
4. Paid tax liens or accounts were placed in the collection more than seven years ago.

11.5.1 Answer key of Quiz Number 5

1) Answer: 1. In exchange for the policyholder's premium payment, the insurer undertakes to pay the policyholder a specified amount in the event of a covered event. This statement accurately describes insurance as a contract where the insurer agrees to provide financial protection to the policyholder in exchange for premium payments.

2) Answer: 2. Benefit recipient. The beneficiary and benefit recipient is the named individual or entity who will receive the death benefit from a life insurance policy.

3) Answer: 3. Lifetime Annuity. A lifetime annuity is an insurance contract that promises to pay the insured a periodic payment based on survival.

4) Answer: 3. The term "credit coverage" is used to describe a subset of life and health insurance that is designed to protect beneficiaries financially by canceling the insured's debts and loans in the event of the insured's death.

5) Answer: 4. Government regulators can specify the pricing for prospective insureds' guaranteed coverages. This option is optional for optimal insurance market competition. Government regulators generally do not specify pricing for insurance products.

6) Answer: 1. The average cost of production for an insurer decreases as production rises. Economies of magnitude occur when the average cost of production decreases as production volume increases.

7) Answer: 3. A company offers identical products at varying prices to distinct groups. Explanation: Price discrimination occurs when a company offers similar products to different groups at varying prices.

8) Answer: 3. Disability insurance benefit triggers include own occupation, but not long-term care. Long-term care insurance policies have an elimination period, the number of days an insured must pay for care following a qualifying claim but before benefits begin (as with a deductible). Long-term care coverage tells an insured how long they'll receive benefits and how much they'll get daily or monthly. Some newer long-term care insurance plans offer lump-sum payouts.

9) Answer: 1. The customer must know more about the insurance company and its products than the insurer (seller). The "lemons" problem occurs when customers have less information than the seller does, leading to adverse selection.

10) Answer: 5. The agent understands their actions better than the principal does; in this case, the insurer does. The principal-agent problem occurs when the agent's interests may not align with the principal's.

11) Answer: 5. Major medical insurance policies usually have high deductibles, although they must state the maximum out-of-pocket expenditures. The elimination phase is not covered by major medical insurance.

12) Answer: 3. State level. State-run insurance departments are primarily responsible for regulating the industry.

13) Answer: 1. The individuals are collecting the information. Applicants for insurance must receive advance notice that includes the type of information to be collected, the sources of information, and the individuals who have access to personal information, but not specifically the individuals collecting the information.

14) Answer: 3. The McCarran-Ferguson Act. The McCarran-Ferguson Act addresses insurance regulation and antitrust laws but does not include provisions safeguarding individual privacy.

15) Answer: 3. Arrests, indictments, or convictions of crime reports. Consumer reporting agencies are not allowed to include information related to arrests, indictments, or convictions of crime reports in their reports.

11.6 Quiz Number 6

1) In most jurisdictions, obtaining a producer's license does not necessitate which of the following?

1. Not have committed any act that is grounds for denial or suspension of an insurance license
2. Be at least 19 years old
3. Pay the required fees
4. Complete any necessary relicensing course

2) In most states, for which of the following an insurance license is required?

1. Rachel, a salaried employee of a large department store chain who advises her employer on insurance-related matters
2. Ross, who works in an advertising agency and oversees the advertising business of a major insurer
3. Phoebe, who works as an underwriter for a small insurer
4. Chandler, who sells insurance only to businesses

3) A person licensed as an insurance producer in another state who transfers to this state has how long after establishing legal residency to become a resident licensee without having to complete relicensing education or an exam?

1. 30 days
2. 60 days
3. 90 days
4. 120 days

4) Which of the following is the least likely to be issued a probationary license?

1. Georgia, whose insurance producer-husband died unexpectedly, leaving her with a business to either learn or sell

2. Kim wants to try selling insurance temporarily before investing the time and money to become licensed

3. Dave, an employee of a business entity, when the individual designated as the licensee in the business entity is disabled and unable to return to work for several months

4. Lee, whose insurance produce-husband passed away unexpectedly, leaving him with a business

5) Business written about the producer's personal life or interests is referred to as:

1. Controlled business

2. Personal business

3. Conflicted business

4. Producer business

6) Which of the following represents an unjust claims practice?

1. Splitting a commission with a prospect

2. Not responding to proof of loss with an affirmation or denial of coverage too quickly

3. Persuading a policyholder to let their current policy expire or be surrendered to purchase a new one

4. Making any untrue, intentionally critical, or damaging statements about another producer, either verbally or in writing

7) An organization that creates model statutes that are frequently adopted by states with minor modifications is:

1. The National Insurance Companies Association

2. The National Independent Commissioners Association

3. The National Association of Insurance Consultants

4. The National Association of Insurance Commissioners

8) The Hoosier Insurance Company employs Ralph as a producer. His Contract allows him to place the company's logo on his business cards and the office entrance. This demonstrates:

1. Express authority
2. Implied authority
3. Persistent implied authority
4. Appearing authority

9) Tom has always required that premium payments be sent to him instead of the insurance. This allows him to track who still needs to pay and contact them personally. His insurer knows about this but hasn't asked him to stop even though it's against the terms of his contract. This is an example of:

1. Express authority
2. Implied authority
3. Persistent implied authority
4. Appearing authority

10) When Gina sells an insurance policy, she collects the first payment and sends it with an application to the insurance provider. Her Contract does not refer to her being responsible for handling any upfront premiums. What this shows is:

1. Express authority
2. Implied authority
3. Persistent implied authority
4. Appearing authority

11) Albert's monthly life insurance premium is due on the tenth of each month. He has always sent the monthly premium late because he is paid at the end of the month. The insurer has accepted this method of payment for three years. A new CEO arrives and resolves to crack down on late premium payments, canceling Albert's policy due to nonpayment. The policy is reinstated after Albert successfully challenges this decision in court. The choice to reinstate the policy is an illustration of:

1. Estoppel
2. Waiver
3. Contract of adhesion
4. Express authorization

12) A producer who acts as an agent on behalf of an insurer is obligated to exercise with the standard of care

1. A licensed insurance agent would be required in a similar scenario
2. One who is reasonable would use it under similar conditions
3. A barrister would apply in comparable circumstances
4. Anyone in comparable circumstances may apply

13) Which component is not essential for formulating a valid contract?

1. Consideration
2. Competent Parties
3. Written Document
4. Legal Objective

14) The initial premium payment submitted with an application comprises which aspect of forming an insurance contract?

1. Consideration
2. Acceptance
3. Offer
4. Legal objective

15) All of the following are part of life insurance contracts, except:

1. The policy folder
2. The insuring clause
3. The conditions
4. The exclusions are not included in life insurance contracts.

11.6.1 Answer key of Quiz Number 6

1) Answer: 2. Be at least 19 years old. Obtaining a producer's license typically requires meeting certain age requirements, paying fees, and completing necessary relicensing courses. The specific age requirement may vary by jurisdiction.

2) Answer: 4. Chandler, who sells insurance only to businesses. In most states, selling insurance to businesses (commercial lines) requires an insurance license.

3) Answer: 3. 90 days. A person licensed as an insurance producer in another state who transfers to a new state has 90 days after establishing legal residency to become a resident licensee without having to complete relicensing education or an exam.

4) Answer: 2. Kim wants to try selling insurance temporarily before investing the time and money to become licensed. Individuals who want to temporarily engage in insurance sales often receive a probationary or temporary license. In this case, Kim's situation aligns with temporary insurance sales.

5) Answer: 1. Controlled business. A business written about the producer's personal life or interests is controlled.

6) Answer: 3. Persuading a policyholder to let their current policy expire or be surrendered to purchase a new one. It is an unfair claims practice to pressure a policyholder into selling another insurance by encouraging them to voluntarily lapse or surrender their current policy.

7) Answer: 4. National Association of Insurance Commissioners. The National Association of Insurance Commissioners (NAIC) creates model statutes frequently adopted by states with minor modifications.

8) Answer: 1. Express authority. Placing the company's logo on business cards and the office entrance is an example of express authority explicitly granted in the producer's contract.

9) Answer: 4. As an example of "appearing authority," consider the fact that Tom's insurer hasn't stopped him from collecting premiums even though doing so constitutes a breach of contract.

10) Answer: 2. Implied authority. Gina acknowledges and applies the initial premium to the insurance company, demonstrating implied authority.

11) Answer: 1. Since Albert had a reasonable expectation that late payments would be tolerated, the insurer's decision to restore the policy is an example of "estoppel," which prevents the insurer from canceling the policy for nonpayment because of the insurer's prior acceptance of late payments.

12) Answer: 2. A reasonable person would apply in comparable circumstances. A producer who acts as an agent on behalf of an insurer is obligated to exercise the same degree of care as a reasonable person would apply in comparable circumstances.

13) Answer: 3. Written Document. While a written document can help establish the terms of a contract, there are other components for formulating a valid contract. Contracts can be oral or implied based on the party's actions.

14) Answer: 1. Consideration. The initial premium payment submitted with an application represents consideration, an essential aspect of forming an insurance contract.

15) Answer: 1. While the terms and exclusions may be outlined in the "policy folder," they are not part of the life insurance contract.

11.7 Quiz Number 7

1) When an insured receives a health insurance policy, how many days does he have to examine it and request a premium refund?

1. 5
2. 10
3. 20
4. 30

2) How lengthy is the benefit period for short-term policies?

1. From 13 to 104 weeks
2. Between 24 and 120 weeks
3. From 12 to 52 weeks
4. From 15 to 130 weeks

3) What sort of health insurance is guaranteed to employees with a group policy if they leave their jobs?

1. Capacity for mobility
2. The COBRA
3. The firm continues to pay insurance premiums.
4. The employee purchases a separate plan.

4) Which of the following is an application component?

1. Attending doctor's report
2. Client investigation
3. Bureau of Medical Information
4. Agent update

5) Which of the following describes a standard risk classification?

1. Uses a Death rate table
2. Adds a surcharge to the premium
3. A lien is imposed on the insurance policy to reduce the coverage amount
4. Individual rating based on age, health, habit, and profession

6) What are the features of term life insurance?

1. It is written for a specific duration
2. Permanent security
3. Creates a currency value
4. Offers permanent protection

7) What is a characteristic of an existence that is adaptable?

1. Durable tenure
2. Modifies the face value of the policy
3. Variable premium
4. Optional death benefit

8) What is a per capita recipient?

1. A group recipient
2. When a recipient is too immature to be eligible
3. When the funds are distributed equally among the recipients
4. The proceeds are distributed to the beneficiary's successors when the beneficiary dies

9) A type of temporary insurance is:

1. Accident insurance
2. A disastrous policy
3. Credit impairment
4. Travel protection

10) Which of the following is not a health policy exclusion?

1. Pre-existing ailments
2. Accidental harm
3. Cosmetic surgery
4. Injury to oneself inflicted on purpose

11) What sort of insurance compensates workers injured while performing their duties?

1. Medicare
2. Medicaid
3. Workers' Compensation
4. Security Benefits

12) Which of the following is not a function of an annuity?

1. The establishment of a fund upon the demise of an individual
2. The replacement of earnings upon the incapacity of an individual
3. The distribution of a lifetime income
4. The reduction of a principal sum to its present value

13) An annuity may be referred to as the inverse of:

1. Compounding
2. Life insurance
3. Retirement planning
4. Social security

14) Annuities are a method for transferring risk to an insurance company and protecting against:

1. Poor investment returns
2. Insurability
3. Depletion of financial resources
4. Demise of a spouse or child

15) The term "minimum return annuity" refers to a type of annuity that ensures

1. An instantaneous annuity
2. A deferred annuity
3. Variable-rate pension
4. A fixed-rate annuity

16) Devon obtains a pension that will provide him with a regular paycheck for the rest of his life, after which he ceases making payments. Devon has acquired:

1. A fixed annuity
2. A linear life annuity
3. A variable annuity
4. A guaranteed temporary annuity

17) Albert has purchased an annuity that will provide him with a monthly income for life. The insurance company has consented to pay the difference to Albert's daughter if he passes away before the Annuity has returned his initial investment. Albert has acquired:

1. A life annuity with no specified period
2. A life annuity with a specified period
3. A refund life annuity
4. A transitory annuity

18) Marcus purchases an annuity with a minimum guaranteed interest rate and protection against principal loss if the contract is held to term. However, if the NASDAQ rises, Marcus's Annuity could accrue more than the minimum guaranteed interest rate. Marcus has acquired a (n).

1. Indexed-equity annuity
2. Annuity indexed to market value
3. Indexed Annuity of market value
4. Equities-adjusted pension

11.7.1 Answer key of Quiz Number 7

1) Answer: 2. 10 days. When an insured receives a health insurance policy, they usually have 10 days to examine it and request a premium refund if they decide not to keep it.

2) Answer: 1. Short-term insurance typically offers protection for anything between three months and two years, with the benefit period ranging from thirteen to 104 weeks.

3) Answer: 2. The COBRA. The Consolidated Omnibus Budget Reconciliation Act allows employees to continue their group health insurance coverage for a certain period after leaving their jobs.

4) Answer: 4. An "Agent update" is a form field in an insurance application that requests information about the policy or insured-party changes, as supplied by the insurance agent.

5) Answer: 4. Individual rating based on age, health, habit, and profession. A standard risk classification involves assessing an individual's risk factors, such as age, health, habits, and profession, to determine their premium rates.

6) Answer: 1. It is written for a specific duration. Term life insurance is written for a specific term or duration, providing coverage for a set period.

7) Answer: 2. In the context of insurance, "modifies the face value of the policy" is indicative of a malleable existence since it indicates that the amount of coverage provided by the policy can be adjusted in response to changes in the policy's circumstances.

8) Answer: 3. When the funds are distributed equally among the recipients. A per capita distribution involves distributing the funds equally among all recipients.

9) Answer: 4. Temporary insurance known as "travel protection" covers unforeseen events including trip cancellations, medical problems, and lost luggage for a set period.

10) Answer: 2. Accidental harm. Health insurance policies typically cover accidental harm, which refers to injuries resulting from accidents. The other options are common exclusions in health policies.

11) Answer: 3. Workers' Compensation. Workers' Compensation insurance compensates injured workers while performing their job duties.

12) Answer: 1. The establishment of a fund upon the demise of an individual. Annuities are primarily designed to provide regular income, not to establish a fund upon an individual's demise.

13) Answer: 1. Compounding. Annuities can be thought of as the inverse of compounding, where regular payments are made instead of accumulating interest over time.

14) Answer: 3. Depletion of financial resources. Annuities are a method for transferring risk to an insurance company to avoid the risk of depleting one's financial resources during retirement.

15) Answer: 4. A fixed-rate annuity. A fixed-rate annuity is a type of annuity that provides a guaranteed minimum rate of return.

16) Answer: 1. A fixed annuity. Devon has obtained a fixed annuity that will provide him with a monthly income for life.

17) Answer: 3. A refund life annuity. Albert has purchased a life annuity with a refund feature, where if he passes away before the annuity returns his initial investment, the difference will be paid to his daughter.

18) Answer: 2. Annuity indexed to market value. Marcus has purchased an indexed annuity that offers a minimum guaranteed interest rate and protection against principal loss, with the potential for higher returns based on the market index.

11.8 Quiz Number 8

1) Eric bought an annuity with favorable interest rates. However, unforeseen circumstances necessitate that he surrender the Annuity. Eric must pay a higher surrender fee if the market has risen than if it has fallen. Eric is the owner of a (n):

1. Equity-indexed pension plan
2. Annuity with market-value adjustments
3. Indexed market-value Annuity
4. Investment-adjusted Annuity

2) Mikaela is the annuitant of an annuity to which she is entitled. Which of the following are unquestionably true in light of this information?

1. Mikaela is contributing to the Annuity
2. Annuity payments will be influenced in part by Mikaela's life expectancy
3. Mikaela is the proprietor of the annuity contract
4. Mikaela will be able to designate a beneficiary for her posthumous benefits

3) Tracey is contributing to an annuity that she believes will support her during her retirement. What is the duration of her current contract?

1. Accumulation Period
2. No forfeiture Period
3. Payout Period
4. Annuity Period

4) Liz invests in an immediate annuity. What is required of the annuity contract?

1. The Annuity must be permanent
2. The Annuity must be variable
3. The Annuity must be deferred
4. The Annuity must have a singular premium

5) Which of the following annuity classes is regulated as security?

1. Fixed annuities

2. Flexible annuities

3. Variable annuities

4. Structured annuities

6) A theory of economic consumption that argues that a household's consumption depends on its income relative to the income of other households with which it is associated is known as:

1. The Hypothesis of Absolute Income

2. The Hypothesis of Efficient Household Income

3. The Hypothesis of Relative Income

4. Life Cycle Hypothesis

5. The Hypothesis of Permanent Income

7) A method by which an insurer can acquire additional capital through the sale and purchase of its insurance by another insurer is known as:

1. Sales of Reversionary Life Insurance

2. Reinsurance

3. Sale/Leaseback Protection

4. Stop Loss Lending Insurance

5. Employ Inverted Capitalization

8) What are actuaries?

1. Establish insurance premiums and reserves based on conservative estimations of potential losses and costs to stay competitive

2. Utilizing the direct writing agency system, sell insurance coverages to prospective clients

3. Determine whether and under what provisions an insurance policy should be issued

4. Negotiate and resolve disputes

5. None of the preceding

9) A representative of an insurance company who decides whether and under what conditions to issue a requested insurance policy is known as:

1. An insurance agent
2. A claims specialist in the insurance industry
3. An underwriter
4. An independent agent
5. None of the Above

10) A danger is:

1. A reason for a loss
2. A physical condition that increases the frequency of loss.
3. A physical condition that increases the severity of loss.
4. A propensity for those with insurance to neglect future loss prevention
5. None of the preceding

11) The objectives of pricing in life and health insurance are:

1. That premium rates should be reasonable
2. That premium should be fair
3. That premium should be excessive
4. All of the above
5. Neither 1 nor 2

12) The method by which insurers determine whether to issue insurance to a person and the parameters of coverage is known as:

1. Insurance Marketing
2. Underwriting
3. Actuarial rate determination
4. Pre-claim settlement pricing
5. None of the above

13) A table that displays the annual probabilities or information regarding health loss for individuals is known as:

1. A Mortality Table
2. An Annuity Table
3. A Morbidity Table
4. Commissioner's Ordinary Life Table
5. U.S. Select Life Table

14) The calculation of rates and values for life and health insurance requires all of the following information, except

1. The likelihood that the insured event will occur
2. Price changes over time
3. The promised benefits
4. Loadings to cover expenses, taxes, profits, and contingencies
5. The insurer's financial strength

15) In life insurance, gross rates are used to recognize:

1. The probability of an insured event
2. Money's worth in terms of time
3. The insurer's financial strength
4. The net rate plus a loading for expenses, contingencies, profits, and taxation
5. The cash surrender value of the policy minus paid-up additions

11.8.1 Answer key of Quiz Number 8

1) Answer: 2. Annuity with market-value adjustments. An annuity with market-value adjustments may have surrender fees that are influenced by changes in the market value of the annuity, resulting in higher fees if the market has risen.

2) Answer: 2. Annuity payments will be influenced in part by Mikaela's life expectancy. Annuity payments are often influenced by the annuitant's life expectancy (Mikaela) and other factors such as the annuity type and payout options.

3) Answer: 1. Accumulation Period. The period when contributions are made to an annuity is known as the accumulation period.

4) Answer: 3. The Annuity must be deferred. An immediate annuity starts paying out soon after the initial premium is paid, while a deferred annuity delays payouts until later.

5) Answer: 3. Variable annuities. Variable annuities are regulated as securities because they involve investment components subject to market fluctuations.

6) Answer: 3. The Hypothesis of Relative Income. The theory of economic consumption that argues that a household's consumption depends on its income relative to the income of other households is known as the Hypothesis of Relative Income.

7) Answer: 2. Reinsurance. Reinsurance is how an insurer can acquire additional capital and spread risk by transferring a portion of its liabilities to another insurer.

8) Answer: 1. D Establish insurance premiums and reserves based on conservative estimations of potential losses and costs to stay competitive. Actuaries are key in determining insurance premiums and reserves based on their analysis of future risks and expenses.

9) Answer: 3. An underwriter. An underwriter is an insurance company representative who decides whether and under what conditions to issue a requested insurance policy.

10) Answer: 1. A reason for a loss is a hazard since the danger signifies a possible source or factor that could result in an unfavorable outcome or injury.

11) Answer: 5. Not 1 or 2 because life and health insurance rates should be actuarially sound, covering predicted expenditures without being excessive or unduly discriminatory.

12) Answer: 2. Underwriting. Underwriting is how insurers determine whether to issue insurance to a person and the coverage parameters.

13) Answer: 3. A Morbidity Table. A table that displays the annual probabilities or information regarding health loss for individuals is known as a Morbidity Table.

14) Answer: 5. If the insurer is financially stable, policyholders can be assured that they will receive their benefits even if the worst should happen, as promised.

15) Answer: 4. The net rate plus a loading for expenses, contingencies, profits, and taxation. Gross rates in life insurance premiums account for the net rate (the basic rate) plus an additional loading to cover various factors such as expenses, contingencies, profits, and taxation.

11.9 Quiz Number 9

1) The 65-year-old insured possesses a non-participating whole-life policy for $100,000. Today, the policy is paid in full. When will the value in cash exceed $100,000?

1. Right now
2. Age 85
3. Not ever
4. Age 100

2) Why is it essential for insurers to have a significant number of similar exposure units?

1. The larger the insured population, the greater the premium collected to cover fixed expenses
2. The insurer's market share grows with every insured
3. The quantity of premiums collected to cover losses is proportional to the number of insured individuals
4. As the number of insureds rises, the insurer's ability to predict losses and calculate premiums becomes more precise

3) Which of the following is false regarding the HICAP program?

1. Health Insurance Counseling Advocacy Program
2. Provides Medicare information to those in need
3. Does not sell or endorse any particular insurance types
4. Provides fee-based assistance based ability to pay

4) In the event of an accidental fatality, the policy's principal amount will be paid:

1. Over a predetermined period
2. On a sliding scale
3. In a single sum
4. Monthly

5) People typically purchase an annuity to secure themselves against the following:

1. Passing away before the mortgage is paid off
2. Becoming uninsurable
3. Outliving their financial means
4. Dying prematurely

6) The guaranteed insurability option permits:

1. In the event of disability, waive premium payments
2. Receive a portion of the mortality benefit in the event of a critical illness
3. Increase the mortality benefit by twofold in the event of an accidental death
4. Get extra coverage whether or not you qualify for insurance

7) Which statement about Medicare Supplement Insurance policies is true?

1. Insurers may only offer comprehensive plans that include primary and supplemental benefits
2. Insurers are unrestricted in their ability to market whichever supplemental coverages they choose
3. Insurers can offer policies with only the essential benefits
4. Insurers may establish insurance policies for the Department of Insurance of California's approval

8) When are parties to a contract required to disclose information based exclusively on their judgment?

1. Only when requested
2. Only when the policy provisions demand it
3. When pertinent
4. Never

9) A disability policy characterized as "guaranteed renewable" is one in which the insurance company

1. Renounces the right to modify the premiums
2. Reserves the right to modify its terms
3. Reserves the right to modify the premiums but cannot alter the policy's terms
4. Cannot renew the policy if the insured ceases to satisfy certain conditions, such as continued employment

10) Loss retention is an effective risk management strategy when all of the conditions listed below are met except for:

1. The loss probability is uncertain.
2. The loss is highly foreseeable
3. The insured elects to assume the associated losses
4. The worst conceivable loss is not significant

11) What happens if the designation of a beneficiary is irrevocable?

1. It cannot be altered without the beneficiary's consent
2. If the irrevocable beneficiary predeceases the insured, all rights revert to the policyholder
3. 1 and 2
4. None

12) X possesses a $25,000 permanent life insurance policy with double indemnity for accidental death. The light aircraft he is piloting crashes into a lake. He is unharmed. He attempts to swim to shore, but misjudgment of the distance leads to his death. His insurer will make the following payment:

1. All of the paid premiums
2. $25,000
3. $50,000
4. $50,000 in addition to all premiums paid
5. None of the preceding

13) Problems associated with minors as beneficiaries can be resolved by:

1. Including a guardian of minor children's property in your will
2. Paying the proceeds into a trust established in the child's name
3. One of 1 or 2
4. None of the preceding

14) From a consumer's perspective, the preferable continuation provisions in a life insurance contract are found in a health insurance policy that is:

1. Can be canceled
2. Voluntarily renewable
3. Renewable subject to conditions
4. Non-cancellable and assuredly renewable
5. None of the preceding

15) Plans for Blue Shield are:

1. Charity organizations
2. Local physicians and their state medical societies provide robust support and control.
3. Plans that provide predominantly coverage for the fees of physicians and surgeons.
4. All of the preceding
5. None of the preceding

11.9.1 Answer key of Quiz Number 9

1) Answer: 4. At age 100, a non-participating whole-life policy's cash value is likely to be greater than the face value (in this case, $100,000).

2) Answer: 4. As the number of insureds rises; the insurer's ability to predict losses and calculate premiums becomes more precise. Many similar exposure units enhance an insurer's ability to predict and spread risk, making premium calculations more accurate.

3) Answer: 4. Provides fee-based assistance based on the ability to pay. Explanation: The Health Insurance Counseling Advocacy Program (HICAP) does not provide fee-based assistance based on the ability to pay; it offers free Medicare information and assistance.

4) Answer: 3. In a single sum. In the event of an accidental fatality, the policy's principal amount is typically paid in a single sum.

5) Answer: 3. Outliving their financial means. People typically purchase an annuity to secure themselves against outliving their financial means, providing a steady income stream in retirement.

6) Answer: 4. Get extra coverage whether or not you qualify for insurance. The guaranteed insurability option allows the insured to purchase additional insurance without proving insurability, typically at predetermined times or life events.

7) Answer: 3. Insurers can offer policies with only the essential benefits. Insurers can offer Medicare Supplement Insurance policies with only the essential benefits, providing consumers with options to choose the coverage that meets their needs.

8) Answer: 4. Unless compelled by the terms of a contract or by applicable rules and regulations, parties to a contract are generally not obligated to divulge information based solely on their judgment.

9) Answer: 3. If you have a disability policy that is "guaranteed renewable," it means that your coverage will stay in effect so long as you continue to pay your payments, and the insurance company can only change the premiums but not the terms of the policy.

10) Answer: 1. Because it requires taking on the potential financial repercussions of a loss without a firm grasp of the risk, loss retention as a risk management method is often ineffective when the loss probability is unknown.

11) Answer: 3. Both (1) and (2) are correct if the beneficiary designation is irrevocable, which means that the beneficiary cannot revoke the designation without the insured's permission, and if the beneficiary dies before the insured, the insured's rights revert to the policyholder.

12) Answer: 2. $25,000. Since X's death resulted from misjudgment and not from an accidental injury as defined by the policy, the insurer will pay the standard death benefit of $25,000.

13) Answer: 3 "One of 1 or 2" is not a suitable solution, but one of the possibilities available may be a trust for the minor beneficiary or a guardian of minor children's property in your will to administer their inheritance.

14) Answer: 5. Consumers desire more solid and consistent life insurance coverage, so none of the above solutions are best for continuation provisions.

15) Answer: 2. Local physicians and their state medical societies provide robust support and control. Plans for Blue Shield involve local physicians and their state medical societies, which provide support and control over the plans' operations and offerings.

11.10 Quiz Number 10

1) A life insurance policy's living benefits are normally obtained through:
1. One-time payment
2. Periodic payments
3. Loan
4. All of the aforementioned
5. 1 and 2

2) The insured person is not involved in choosing how an insurance contract is worded. Insurance contracts are regarded as _____ in this regard.
1. Contracts by Regulation
2. Contracts of Adhesion
3. Contracts of Forbearance
4. Contracts by Law

3) The insurance company's declaration in an insurance contract, known as a(n) _____, lays forth the fundamental component of insurance, which is to compensate for damages covered by the policy.
1. Designation of beneficiary
2. Amount of premium
3. Insuring clause
4. Rider

4) Which of these does not constitute health insurance?
1. Dental coverage
2. Insurance for vision
3. Insurance against disability
4. Insurance for long-term care
5. Neither of the above

5) A commercial customer is trying to find methods to lower its monthly insurance costs. The agent understands they need to switch to a high deductible health plan to reach the desired premium amount set by the firm. What should you cover in your discussion as part of your advice to the company?

1. POS
2. HMO
3. PPO
4. HSA

6) Under the Financial Modernization Act, a person about whom a financial institution obtains information is classified as a:

1. Customer
2. Consumer
3. Client
4. Patron

7) Ted, a health insurance agent, used the prospect of a weekend getaway to a nearby resort as bait to get a potential customer to buy a policy from him. What is the name for this if it is not acceptable?

1. Dismissed; Fabrication
2. False—Twisting
3. It's totally fine to do so
4. No; Discounting

8) The Commissioner of Insurance has the following powers:

1. Carrying out probes and analyses
2. Making rules and regulations that make sense
3. Promulgating insurance law
4. Certification of state-issued insurance policy forms
5. All of the above

9) The insurance department's non-financial regulation operations can be classified as:

1. Market regulation
2. Conduct regulation
3. Market conduct
4. Insurance conduct

10). What refers to a group formed to safeguard the interests of annuitants, policyholders, & creditors of bankrupt insurance companies?

1. Insurance Companies
2. Departmental Organizations
3. Limited Liability Companies
4. Guaranty Association

11) Ken has only paid four premiums on his health insurance policy when a vehicle strikes him. The insurance company covers his treatment and extended stay in intensive care to nearly 500,000 dollars. This demonstrates:

1. Contract of Adhesion
2. Lavatory Contract
3. Unilateral Contract
4. Contract of the Highest Good Faith

12) Carol applies for life insurance and pays the initial premium. She now holds:

1. Accepted an offer from the insurer
2. Made an offer to the insurer
3. Accepted a counteroffer from the insurer
4. Made a counteroffer to the insurer

13) After reviewing Carol's application, the insurer proposed a new policy with terms she did not approve of, such as an exclusion. The insurance company has:

1. Accepted an offer from Carol
2. Made an offer to Carol
3. Carol's counteroffer and decided to accept it
4. Presented Carol with a counteroffer

14) The omission of disclosing known facts is:

1. False Representation
2. Concealment
3. Fraud
4. Imitation

15) All of the following statements are motivations for purchasing term life insurance, except for:

1. Survivor security
2. Estate planning
3. Investment Income
4. Land preservation

11.10.1 Answer key of Quiz Number 10

1) Answer: 5. Life insurance living benefits can be taken out in one lump sum or regular installments. The insured may utilize this cash to pay monthly bills with the installment method.

2) Answer: 2. Unless the language used is obliged to be stated in a precise way by law, a court will construe the language used in a contract negatively if it contains ambiguous phrasing.

3) Answer: 3. In return for the premium and the insured's adherence to the policy's conditions, the insurer agrees to pay for any losses that occur.

4) Answer: 5. There are many different kinds of health insurance coverage, including those listed above.

5) Answer: 4. HSAs are utilized with high-deductible health plans. An HSA lets you save insurance premiums and spend them on medical expenses. HSA account assets can be utilized for medical services; thus, participants commonly use them for uninsured expenses like chiropractic treatments.

6) Answer: 1. Customer. Under the Financial Modernization Act, a person about whom a financial institution obtains information is classified as a customer.

7) Answer: 4. The term "rebate" refers to an incentive offered to a potential insurance buyer. As an example of unfair competition, it is illegal. A second instance is when the agent's commission is deducted from the applicant's policy premium.

8) Answer: 5. All of the options are correct. The head of the Department of Insurance has the authority to promulgate insurance law, examine and authorize insurance policy forms used inside the state, and conduct investigations and examinations.

9) Answer: 2. Conduct regulation. Conduct regulation is a catch-all term for the insurance department's non-financial regulating actions that guarantee honest dealings and ethical behavior.

10) Answer: 4. Guaranty associations. Associations set up to safeguard policyholders, annuitants, claimants, and creditors of financially insolvent insurers are called guaranty associations. These associations provide a safety net in case an insurer becomes insolvent.

11) Answer: 2. This arrangement is an example of a "Lavatory Contract," in which the insurer offers coverage and pays the insured's medical bills even though the insured (Ken) has paid only four premiums.

12) Answer: 2. Made an offer to the insurer. Carol's act of applying for life insurance and paying the initial premium is considered making an offer to the insurer.

13) Answer: 4. Presented Carol with a counteroffer. The insurer is modifying the policy and including an exclusion constitutes a counteroffer to Carol.

14) Answer: 2. Concealment. Explanation: The omission of disclosing known facts is called concealment, which can affect the validity of an insurance contract.

15) Answer: 3. Investment Income. Term life insurance is typically purchased for survivor security, estate planning, and other financial protection purposes. It is not primarily purchased for investment income.

CONCLUSION

___

You have successfully navigated the "Life and Health Insurance License Exam Guide." In reaching this conclusion, you have not only acquired a thorough comprehension of the insurance industry's essential concepts but also developed the skills and strategies necessary to excel on your licensing examination.

Throughout this guide, we have traversed the complex landscape of life and health insurance, delving into fundamental principles, policy nuances, regulatory frameworks, ethical considerations, and exam strategies. Your commitment to acquiring this knowledge demonstrates your dedication to a career that has the potential to significantly affect the financial security and well-being of individuals.

As you prepare for the licensing exam, keep in mind that this guide is more than a source of information; it is a tool that enables you to confidently approach the exam, answer difficult questions, and demonstrate your knowledge of the subject matter. Embrace the practice opportunities, hone your test-taking strategies, and rely on the industry's ethical principles.

Your journey as a licensed insurance professional begins after the exam. You are about to enter a dynamic field in which your expertise will assist clients in securing their futures, making informed decisions, and protecting the well-being of their loved ones. The information in these pages will continue to serve as a valuable resource as you pursue this rewarding career path.

Remember that the insurance industry's foundation is trust, honesty, and a dedication to excellence. If you uphold these principles, your commitment to professionalism and ethical behavior will set you apart in a competitive landscape.

As you close this chapter, embrace your newfound confidence and knowledge. The "Life and Health Insurance License Exam Guide" has been your companion in preparation; now it is your turn to take charge and embark on your path to success. We wish you success as

a respected insurance professional in your examination and future endeavors. Your journey has just begun, and we are confident you will leave a positive and enduring mark on the life and health insurance industry.

GLOSSARY

1. **Accelerated Death Benefit:** A clause that allows the insured to receive a portion of the lump sum in advance in case of terminal illness.

2. **Accidental Death Benefit:** An additional benefit paid to the beneficiary if the insured's death results from an accident.

3. **Annuity:** A financial product that provides regular payments to an individual over a specified period, often used as a retirement income source.

4. **Annuity Payout Options:** In various ways, annuity payments can be received, such as a lump sum, fixed period, or life annuity.

5. **Assignment:** The transfer of the rights or benefits of an insurance policy to another person or entity.

6. **Beneficiary:** The person or entity designated to receive the benefits or proceeds of an insurance policy upon the occurrence of a specified event, such as the insured's death.

7. **Cash Surrender Value:** The amount of cash that can be obtained by surrendering a permanent life insurance policy before its maturity or death benefit payout.

8. **Cash Value:** The savings component of a permanent life insurance policy that accumulates over time and can be accessed by the policyholder.

9. **Claim:** A formal request by the policyholder or beneficiary for payment of benefits under the insurance policy.

10. **Coinsurance:** The percentage of costs shared between the insurance company and the insured after the deductible is met.

11. **Copayment:** A fixed amount the insured pays for covered services, typically used in health insurance.

12. **Death Benefit:** The money paid to the beneficiary upon the insured's death under a life insurance policy.

13. **Deductible:** The amount of money the insured must pay out of pocket before the insurance coverage starts.

14. **Exclusion:** Specific situations or conditions that are not covered in the insurance policy.

15. **Grace Period:** The period after the premium due date when the policy remains in force, even if the premium is unpaid.

16. **Guaranteed Minimum Income Benefit (GMIB):** A rider that guarantees a minimum income level from an annuity, regardless of market performance.

17. **Guaranteed Renewable:** A feature in health insurance policies that guarantees the policy's renewal as long as premiums are paid, regardless of changes in health.

18. **Insured:** The person whose life is covered by a life insurance policy or who receives health insurance coverage.

19. **Living Benefit:** An option that allows the policyholder to access part of the lump sum in the event of death while still alive in case of terminal illness or other qualifying conditions.

20. **Long-Term Care Insurance:** Coverage that helps individuals pay for long-term care services, such as nursing home care or home health care.

21. **Medicare:** Medicare is a federal health insurance plan for those 65 and up and some younger people with disabilities.

22. **Medicaid:** A state-funded and federally-funded program that offers low-income people and families that qualify for health insurance.

23. **Policyholder:** The individual who owns an insurance policy and has the rights and responsibilities associated with it.

24. **Policy Lapse:** Terminating an insurance policy due to non-payment of premiums.

25. **Policy Loan:** A loan taken out by the policyholder using the cash value of a permanent life insurance policy as collateral.

26. **Premium:** The amount of money the policyholder pays to the insurance company in exchange for insurance coverage.

27. **Pre-existing Condition:** A health condition that existed before the insurance coverage started and may impact coverage or premium rates.

28. **Premium Waiver:** A rider that waives premium payments if the insured becomes disabled or meets certain criteria.

29. **Reinstatement:** Restoring a lapsed insurance policy to its original status after the policyholder pays the required premiums.

30. **Rider:** An optional provision added to an insurance policy that provides additional coverage or benefits beyond the standard terms.

31. **Suicide Clause:** A clause in a life insurance policy that limits or excludes coverage for death by suicide within a specified period after the policy's issuance.

32. **Term Conversion:** The possibility of transforming a term life insurance policy into a permanent life insurance policy without undergoing a new medical examination.

33. **Term Life Insurance:** Life insurance provides cover for a specific duration or period with no cash value accumulation.

34. **Underwriting:** Evaluating an applicant's risk factors to determine the premium rate and insurability.

35. **Underinsured:** When an insurance policy's coverage amount is insufficient to fully cover the incurred loss.

36. **Universal Life Insurance:** A flexible type of permanent life insurance that allows policyholders to adjust their premium payments and death benefits.

37. **Waiver of Premium for Disability:** A provision that exempts the policyholder from paying premiums if they become disabled and unable to work.

38. **Whole Life Insurance:** Permanent life insurance that offers coverage for the insured's entire lifetime and includes a cash value component.

Made in the USA
Columbia, SC
10 March 2025

54986834R00076